140 ULTIMATE TWITTER LOLS
NAIL SOCIAL MEDIA, THE FUNNY WAY

140 ULTIMATE TWITTER LOLS

NAIL SOCIAL MEDIA, THE FUNNY WAY

@SedgeBeswick

2014

First Printing: 2014

ISBN 978-1-326-04194

Sedge Beswick
ASOS Ltd. Greater London House
London, NW1 7FB

www.sedgebeswick.com

For Jeevan.
After all – you're the only person in the world
to have won a #BeswickBAFTA for your tweeting.

Contents

Introduction

Twitter, like all social media channels, is a constantly evolving platform. There isn't a single rule that applies to everyone – except to always have as much fun with it as possible, and keep your mind open to learning new tips and tricks to engage your followers along the way.

Whether you're on Twitter as a soul operator, or as the resident social whiz kid at a brand, the key, as this book attests, is to keep pace with the platform's ever-changing features and the appetite of your audience. Ultimately, keeping things fresh and rolling with the punches is key.

In keeping with Twitter's 140-character limit, I wanted to pull out the strongest 140 characters at large on there, and examine how they've racked up such huge followings and engagement rates. Many have stuck two fingers up to the principles of good social media practise to achieve Twitter stardom – but as the saying goes: 'you can't make an omelette without breaking a few eggs'. And it's these rule breakers that are my personal favourites.

While taking in the LOLs, hopefully you'll learn a few things. And if you don't, well, that's OK, too.

With a bit of luck, after reading this, you'll be able to turbo boost your Twitter account and cultivate a loyal band of followers. If Twitter ever increases its character limit from 140 characters, and I need to extend my book, let's hope your newly beefed up account makes it into the next edition ;)

And, naturally, I've probably forgotten/missed/never heard of some of the best accounts out there, so if you've got any great ones, tweet me: @SedgeBeswick or use the hashtag #TwitterLOLs.

Happy reading...

A few quick points before you start:

1. I do not own the tweets called out in this book. The author of these tweets is clearly reference at the top of each entry.

2. Follower count: this was done at the time of completing the book, which was the end of September 2014. They will be out of date at the time of reading, but should give you a rough idea... another great thing about social.

3. Suspended accounts: at the time of writing a few of the accounts had been suspended. By the time you're reading it (right now – hi there!), there will likely be a few additional accounts that have been   suspended. Even though they don't exist, hopefully you'll still be able to learn from them.

140 ULTIMATE TWITTER LOLS

1.
The Rule Breakers

Forget everything you thought you knew about social media etiquette. These Twitter handles are so wrong, they're right.

1.
@Big_Ben_Clock
Founded: October 2009
Following: 450,715

The world of social media constantly challenges you to think of funny, timely and relevant bits of content that engage your community. It's about having your finger on the pulse: what's trending? What's your customer talking about? What are they buying? Where are they right now? Thinking of new ways to entertain and connect with them is tough, but, sometimes, simplicity really is the answer.

First up, we have one of my favourite Twitter accounts, and one that has simplicity at its core: @Big_Ben_Clock. If Big Ben had a voice, what would it say? Of course, the Palace of Westminster's Great Bell already has a voice, of sorts, and chimes every hour, on the hour, all day, all year. And so does its Twitter account. Every hour, on the hour, all day, all year @Big_Ben_Clock tweets 'DONG DONG DONG DONG DONG DONG DONG DONG'.

Whoever decided to take Big Ben online and publish hourly tweets deserves some serious kudos for that innovative thinking. I don't know who you are, but this is social media at its finest – simple, sharable and witty.

The result? It's one of the most retweeted accounts out there. Who wouldn't laugh quietly to themselves every time they see that barmy string of 'DONGS' in their newsfeed? After all, some poor sod has to schedule all those, like clockwork (if you pardon the pun).

Tip: To help to continue the dialogue, schedule some of your tweets in advance. This will save you heaps of time.

2.
@TheBatman
Founded: March 2010
Following: 479,428

The anti-hero whose weapons include super human strength and sharp one-liners, @TheBatman mixes up real world goings-on with the odd Gotham City reference – and it totally works.

Previously known as @God_Damn_Batman, he's now simplified his name and upped the arrogance factor; he goes against all the basic DOs of Twitter (he's never retweeted, favourited or followed anyone), yet still his following grows.

Here are a few tweets that prove how a few compellingly cocky tweets can be the key to success online:

•Sometimes I watch that Ben Affleck Daredevil movie before going out on patrols. Then let the rage do the rest.
•When in doubt, Batman.
•When life gives you lemons, be thankful it's just lemons. Life could have shot both your parents in a dirty alley when you were 8.

Tip: When you're trying to build your profile on Twitter, follow people who help to tell your story, people who are relevant to you, and who you can start conversations with as like minded people. The 'go it alone' approach of @TheBatman doesn't usually work!

4

3.
@Coffee_Dad
Founded: March 2012
Following: 133,216

What's funny about a coffee-loving dad with access to a smartphone and a Twitter account? Well, at face value, absolutely nothing. But one brief swipe through @Coffee_Dad's account and you'll be hooked harder than he is on double espressos.

Like all Twitter rule-breakers, he turns a dry subject matter into something people actually give a shit about – in his case, when and where he takes his latest cup of Joe.

Among all the coffee stuff, however, emerges a darker story. @Coffee_Dad occasionally tweets about his dead son, and claims he uses coffee as a coping mechanism. If this were a genuine account, this would obviously be really tragic. But the fact that this is, in all likelihood, a spoof account, there's actually something quite funny about this macabre, seemingly impulsive outpourings of emotion.

Tip: Find a common topic and make it your own to become instantly relatable whilst it might sound boring at first, there's always a way to make it engaging.

4.
@Joey7Barton
Founded: July 2010
Following: 2,726,167

Ah, a Footballer. @Joey7Barton, ex-MCFC which as a @MCFC fan makes me want to go easy on him but, I can't! Barton is one of those people that you follow and find funny, for all the wrong reasons. Twitter likes to disagree and shame him for, well, every tweet. And unfortunately, it's all very well deserved.

He isn't the most lovable of guys; he has quite the reputation and in true Barton style, he's controversial.

His tweeting highlight really does have to be the time he tweeted saying "I'd destroy both the midfielders Spurs have wasted money on and I'm a championship player. Albeit, an exceptional one...". With over 2K Retweets, it went viral, only for Barton to backtrack when he got a hammering at Spurs losing 4-0. And, in true social-style, people were quick to comment on his ridiculous tweet... he was owned, left, right and center. This, of course, is the main reason why Barton has made into #TwitterLOLs.

Follow Barton for playground-esq arguments, Twitter storms and all round, nonsense.

And to think, Footballers have a bad name, eh?

Tip: Think before you tweet.

5.
@OneTweetTony
Founded: June 2012
Following: 2,613

@OneTweetTony does exactly what it says on the tin. He's been on Twitter since 2012 and has tweeted once: 'Nailed it. That's a wrap!'

Strong LOL game.

Follow him to see if he stays true to his word, or if he caves under the pressure of his thousands of followers and tweets again. I love how this one goes against what we're told while we bash our heads thinking of new content ideas each day.

Tip: Stay true to your word, do what you say you'll do on Twitter.

6.
@I_AM_NIGEL
Founded: March 2011
Following: 920

Have you ever been in one of those arguments where the other person says 'I completely agree' to absolutely everything? You call them an arsehole, to which they say 'Yup, that's me'. It's frustrating; all you want is a reaction, and that's the last thing you get.

Interacting with @I_AM_NIGEL should evoke similar feelings, but he's also pretty darn funny. All he replies to any tweet or direct message that comes his way is 'I AM NIGEL'. He never steers away from what he knows, and what he knows is that he is Nigel.

This account is totally bonkers and, all in all, pretty pointless. But it's an instant pick me up.

Tweet him and see if you can find out anything else about @I_AM_NIGEL. He's probably a real talker once you get him going...

Tip: Sometimes you have to be a little whacky to stand out on Twitter.

7.
@AdviceMallards
Founded: March 2011
Following: 202,526

Meet Dave. He's a duck. But he's no ordinary duck – he's a mallard who's made a name out of quacking pearls of wisdom online.

Whether it's relationship advice or a handy 'how to' guide, this bird has it covered. Forget talking to your pals for tips and tricks, turn your attention to @AdviceMallards instead.

The lesson here is not to believe everything you read – sometimes Dave's advice is a bit ropey. Check out some of his less helpful life hacks below:

- Tall people are aware that they are tall. They don't need you to remind them every time you see them.
- If you're trying to quit smoking, go to a sauna 3 days in a row. You'll sweat out the nicotine and it'll be easier to quit.
- Summer is hot. Winter is cold. You know this was coming, stop whining about it.

Tip: You'll hear 'if it's not useful, don't tweet it, A LOT' – this one ruins that example but it's consistent, which will always work.

8.
@Countingcrows_

Founded: April 2012
Following: 3,041

Can you guess what @CountingCrows_ does? Oh, you can... *claps*.

Gone are the travails of counting sheep to send you to the land of nod. Now you can just fire up Twitter and join this guy in crow-counting to combat sleepless nights.

It goes a little like this:

• 50 crows
• 49 crows
• 48 crows

You get the drift (see what I did there?)

Tip: Sometimes, weird works. Again, this goes against everything we're taught when you're told to think of new and engaging ways to communicate with your fans.

9.
@b0ringtweets

Founded: May 2013
Following: 222,843

The two main ways of successfully engaging an audience on Twitter are story telling and relevance. This account defies both of those, but nails it anyway.

This feed does something really clever with the average Twitter user's propensity to overshare and detail his or her every move. It devotes itself to dull 'revelations', such as 'I had half a shandy last night. I still feel a bit drunk now. Never again.'

For anyone who follows @B0ringTweets and finds themselves reading a tweet similar to something they've shared at some point, take note: no one cares whether you just coughed or what time you woke up.

Here are some of @b0ringtweets best banalities:

- I'm eating some toast. It's crazy to think that it was officially classed as bread just 7 minutes ago.
- Arctic Monkeys are not monkeys, nor do they come from the polar region. Please RT to raise awareness. Thank you
- Germany were winning 1-0, then they were winning 2-0, then they were winning 3-0, then they were winning 4-0, now they are winning 5-0.

Tip: C'mon - don't be the person on Twitter that @b0ringtweets tweets. If you wouldn't say it to your mates in the pub, don't say it on Twitter.

10.
@EveryWord
Founded: November 2007
Following: 90,585

It's such a shame that this Twitter account's project completed earlier this year, because it was such an innovative (and interesting) use of the platform. As its name suggests, @EveryWord simply and hilariously tweeted every single recorded word in the English language.

Needless to say, 'sex' was heavily retweeted, with over 3,000 people picking up on the random nature of this expertly executed project.

It's simple and equally amusing to see single words getting such immense pick up..

Tip: Don't overthink it – there's a place for just about everything on Twitter. The simplest ideas are usually the best.

11.
@KurtQuote
Founded: August 2012
Following: 8,366

With a handle like @KurtQuote, one might expect this account to do one thing: tweet quotes from Nirvana front man Kurt Cobain.

In reality, it tweets fabricated quotes, with made up dates. Why? Because, for whatever reason, it aims to do nothing more than rile Cobain's diehard fans. It's like trolling in reverse.

Call it bad taste, but the real hilarity comes with reading the replies to these tweets. Cobain's fans don't just get ticked off; they are full on outraged by these tweets, and the audacity of the person behind them.

This account sticks two fingers up to the principles of being useful or insightful on Twitter. And in turn, it's grown an enormous following.

Tip: Don't believe everything you read on Twitter. It's best to check your facts before you repeat or retweet.

2.

Nailing the Basics

These accounts will have you in stitches, and school you in innovative ways to grow your following, get more retweets, and unlock your true Twitter potential.

12.
@SusanBoyle
Founded: September 2009
Following: 20,955

Remember when @SusanBoyle invited her followers to attend an Anal Bum Party?

Of course, SuBo wasn't actually inviting her fans for an afternoon of playful bum fun at her West Loathian home. Thank goodness. In reality, someone in her social team forgot to check whether the hashtag for her album launch could be misinterpreted. They failed to recognise that with a slight change in capitalisation, #SusanAlbumParty becomes #SusAnalBumParty.

Naturally, it got quite the pick up and quite frankly, I couldn't publish half the tweets that were sent with the hashtag in this book.

Tip: Capitalisation doesn't matter on Twitter. If you use names or hashtags, you can use any sequence of capitalisation. However, consistency is best when it comes to your communication. So this book will always be referred to as #TwitterLOLs, even though #TWITTERLOLS or #TwitterLOLS does the same job.

13.
@PizzaHutCares
Founded: May 2013
Following: 1,584

It's easy to say you care, even if you don't. @PizzaHutCares' approach to online customer service is a sound example of that.

Here's how the Hut fobbed off one peckish customer's complaint:

Customer: "Terrible service from @PizzaHunt. Ordered before halftime of NE game. Still not here." The reply? "We always want to deliver for you in a timely manner. Visit *https://pizzahut.com/phcares* and share details of your experience."

For one, if your customers come to you on Twitter, respond on that platform – don't send them elsewhere. Second, be useful. This is nothing more than a copy and paste job.

There's plenty of alternative routes that they could have gone down here: openly apologized, taken the details to check the status of the pizza, offered a coupon or the pizza for free as an apology. Instead, they literally did nothing.

The plus, is that they actually responded. Silence is never the card to play.

Tip: Twitter and customer service go hand in hand - make it personalised, make it fun.

14.
@EmrgencyKittens
Founded: December 2012
Following: 530,921

Thinking of fresh material that will engage your followers is time consuming, and can be a thankless task.

The great thing about social media, however, is that you can see immediately whether something has resonated with your community; it gives you the power to adapt and be reactive. You no longer have to wait for days, weeks or months to gain insight into what works, which means you can shape your content plan a lot more easily.

Right now, if your social output involves cats, you're onto a good thing. The Internet has gone cat crazy, and is overrun with feline-centric social accounts, memes, and, of course, the nyan cat. That's what makes @EmrgencyKittens so great: it's relevant, topical, and pretty darn cute to boot.

It dispenses kitten pics all day long. A simple strategy, which brightens newsfeeds, one tabby at a time.

Tip: Got an important tweet (or cat!) to share? Tweet it more than once, with different angle to cover all time zones.

15.
@OctoberJones
Founded: December 2009
Following: 93,539

When Twitter gave its users the option of adding media, including emojis, pictures and video to their tweets, this had a knock on effect on engagement levels, which soared 155%[1].

With that in mind, it should come as no surprise that clever illustrator @OctoberJones is smashing it on Twitter. He publishes reactive drawings in response to things happening around world and online; in doing so, he captures the collective sentiment of his followers and the wider social community, and reaps the rewards of publishing timely, engaging content – which just so happens to be a flip load of retweets and favourites.

Like him, you can tap into the lives of your followers and react to trending topics with mega-shareable content. Just make sure to put your own spin on events and join the conversation while it's fresh. There's nothing worse than seeing a brand or individual putting their two cents in when all of the good jokes have already been made.

Tip: Think visual – you'll see higher engagement.

---

[1] Sprinklr, 2014

16.
@AliceWhitey

Founded: December 2011
Following: 17,574

If you've ever sat in a room with me for more than 30 seconds, you'll realise that I'm an oversharer. Provided it's a story about something deeply personal, embarrassing or downright gross, I'll happily share it with you. That's why I love Alice White – because she does all that, but broadcasts it to thousands on Twitter.

White lives the life of a typical twenty-something: it's disorganised, chaotic and, of course, there's the odd relationship drama or two. Sure, I've never met her, and she could be the most balanced chick out there, but we'll pretend that everything you see on Twitter is 100% true; effectively, her newsfeed reads like a more relatable version of the Daily Mail's sidebar of shame.

Brutally and refreshing honest, White has a no holds barred approach to Twitter and thinks nothing of telling it exactly how it is. There's something pretty inspiring about a young woman willing girls all over the globe to follow her lead and be themselves – no matter how shambolic that self may be.

Tip: Be honest and human – Twitter is transparent.

17.
@TescoMobile

Founded: April 2009
Following: 73,279

@TescoMobile is the proud owner of my all-time favourite Twitter conversation, if you missed it, here is a snippet:

- @RealJaffaCakes BREAKING NEWS: We just found your Jaffa 'cakes' in the sweet biscuit aisle. You're living a lie. #NoJoke

I won't lie, there's plenty of speculation as to whether that conversation was genuine or whether it was set up my a group of nerdy Social Media Managers but you know what? Who gives a shit! It was brilliant.

Whenever I'm training people on the engagement side of social I always use @TescoMobile as an example of an account that they should aspire to and of course, follow.

They're not the best of networks out there, (they know that!) so they have to gain awareness and trust elsewhere. And that, my friend, is what social media is all about. (That and the two-way dialogue.) The quicker you can reply, the better. The more relevant your reply, the better. The more personalised, the better. The wittier your reply, the more sharable it is.

Tesco are quick, and instantly witty making their brand lovable which is why people will get a contract with them.

Tip: Service Level Agreement's (SLA) are super important, if you're a brand – the lower the better! It'll help with the two way dialogue.

18.
@KngHnryVIII
Founded: November 2010
Following: 36,634

A serial monogamist with a penchant for beheadings may not sound like someone to base a parody Twitter account on. But even to someone who knows as little about Tudor history as me, Henry VIII cuts a rather intriguing figure, whose existence is ripe with moments to get a good LOL out of (once you look beyond all that grisly guillotine stuff).

If I were to think about ol' Henry in a modern world, I imagine he'd be pretty similar to how he was back in the day. You know, a man who likes his bacon, drinks his weight in beer on the reg, and ensures he always dripping with swag. And that's basically the character this parody Twitter account depicts.

@KngHnryVIII brings the iconic king into the 21st century; they've made him accessible and relatable, while offering the odd factual titbit. As all good accounts should, this one ticks all the Es of social media: it's entertaining, educational, and engaging.

Also check out @WWM_Shakesphere if you like this one.

Tip: Engage, entertain and then, educate.

19.
@BobbyFinger

Founded: February 2009
Following: 12,602

If a quality meme or gif is your thing, then look no further than @BobbyFinger.

Bobby's a great observer of pop culture, and knows how to spin the kind of celebrity-centric nonsense that goes viral in the blink of an eye.

While I can't add GIFs or YouTube videos into this book, I can share my all time favourite tweet from @BobbyFinger:

• "Of all the horrifying noises I could hear in the public bathroom, I think the absolute worst was the iPhone shutter."

Tip: Think about the Internet. If your pals are talking about it/sharing it – it's probably a trend and you'll reap the benefits of talking about it.

Use your timeline and your pals as a guide.

20.
@USAirlines
Founded: June 2009
Following: 519,469

As you probably know by now, the key to nailing social media is reacting to events at breakneck speeds. But when you're trying to keep pace like this, mistakes happen.

The best way to rectify these mistakes is fess up and admit fault. That way, you'll win back the trust of your community. Something that @USAirlines knows only too well...

This airline makes #TwitterLOLs because they once tweeted an extremely explicit picture in response to a customer complaint. While the picture went viral, and everyone online was laughing, @USAirlines were trying to avert a PR disaster.

But they abided by the 'honesty is the always the best policy' mantra, and revealed that this photo had first been sent to @USAirlines, and was only posted out from its feed because someone in its social team was attempting to report it as inappropriate.

Tip: Always re-read your tweets before you hit send. While manning the @ASOS feed, I accidently put 'bottom' rather than 'borrow'. Sure, that doesn't sound too bad when you look at it in isolation, but when you put it in a sentence like this... 'Cute #ASOS jeans! LOVE your dog too, can we bottom him?' it's pretty awkward.

21.
@NicoleCrother
Founded: ACCOUNT CLOSED
Following: ACCOUNT CLOSED

Social media is open, so don't tweet anything from your personal account that could land you in hot water if read by the wrong person.

@NicolaCrowther, who was working on the TV series @Glee, tweeted a spoiler that revealed the identity of the prom king and queen in one episode. The Executive Producer of the show, @BFalchuk, was among the seriously pissed off people who saw her tweet, and he replied with 'hope you're qualified to do something besides work in entertainment'. ***Bows head in shame***

@NicoleCrowther was apparently fired and learned the hard way that what you say on Twitter can cost you your job. There is a lot of speculation around whether or not this was a PR stunt to get a bit of traction for the show, but it's still worth bearing in mind.

Tip: Here are a few ways to keep your work and Twitter relationship a harmonious one:

• If you're off 'sick', don't post updates about the great day you're having, or even get tagged on someone else's page.
• Most bosses encourage social behaviour, but still, don't post excessively at work.
• Don't tweet about job offers or interviews before that contract is signed or your notice handed in.
• Check which account you're logged into before you post.

22.
@Waitrose
Founded: June 2009
Following: 162,698

A great way to engage your Twitter community is with a super simple 'fill in the blank'.

@Waitrose tried this with a "Fill in the blank: I shop at Waitrose because ___".

What could possibly go wrong...

@Waitrose is the most upscale of all Britain's supermarkets, and is famously the posh person's retailer. So, unsurprisingly, some of the 'blanks' people tweeted back picked up on the snob-factor associated with the brand. Here are a few of the finest ones:

- I shop at Waitrose because I'm filthy rich and therefore automatically better than you are.
- I shop at Waitrose because their swan burgers are good enough for the queen.
- I shop at Waitrose because Asda Value foie gras just won't do

Whether this campaign royally backfired or proved that Waitrose is leagues ahead of its competitors, such as @Tesco and @Sainsbury's, is open for debate.

Tip: Have you thought about your contingency plan? You need to be ready to respond to your customers; rain or shine.

23.
@AnthonyWeiner
Founded: January 2013
Following: 23,949

Most days, there's an item in the news reporting the latest social media sex scandal. Whether it's teens using Snapchat to exchange naughty pics or celebrities' iCloud accounts getting hacked for nude pictures, the social space has become a somewhat salacious place.

But what happened when an American politician decided to get involved in the trend?

When (former) New York Congressman @AnthonyWeiner went to send a Direct Message via Twitter, he accidentally sent it to all of his followers. Things could be worse, but maybe not when the contents of that message mirror the contents of your pants. Yup, that's right, Weiner accidentally published a dick pic.

Naturally, his political career deflated almost as quickly as his erection.

Tip: Whether you want to send photos like this privately or not, think about where these images could go if they end up in the wrong hands. The easiest way to avoid a cock up like Weiner's is to not send nudey pics in the first place. But if you really want to, double check your settings AND double check who you're sending things to.

24.
@RobinThicke
Founded: May 2007
Following: 1,146,789

There are loads of clever ways for celebrities and brands to narrow the distance between themselves and their audience: for instance, Q&A sessions on Twitter. However, if you're a divisive figure, like Blurred Lines singer @RobinThicke, whose lyrics are widely considered to be the misogynistic ramblings of a one-hit wonder, holding a Q&A is fraught with danger... Something he discovered to his detriment when he asked people to submit their questions using #AskThicke.

Here are a just few of the tweets he received:

• #AskThicke Did you really write a rape anthem as a love song for your wife and are you still wondering why she left you?
• How many naked women did it take before you stopped seeing them as people & instead saw them as YouTube hits? #AskThicke
• How often should I delete my internet search history? You strike me as a good person to ask. #AskThicke

The lesson? It's great giving real people access but, and it's a big but, be mindful of the brand or artist's reputation. If it's not good, there's no way a Q&A can go to plan or change people's minds.

Tip: Think of the questions people might raise, and ask yourself if it's worth that negativity being heightened further by asking people to express them openly on Twitter.

25.
@KeynoteScarf

Founded: September 2014
Following: 1,173

At the time of writing this entry, Apple announced the iPhone 6: a momentous occasion for all in the tech and social media universe. Kinda.

But this year, it wasn't just news of Apple's latest handset and watch that went viral. The keynote speechmaker's scarf was so sartorially questionable that it started trending, too.

Here are a few examples of how it went down:

- @MarkDorison: I'm dressing up as scarf guy for Halloween
- @StephMBuck: The live stream is down but the most important question is how many more people will wear purple? #AppleLive

Brands, fans, and haters – they all got involved and, quicker than the time it takes to say iScarf, a parody account was born.

Here's what it tweeted: PAY ATTENTION TO ME #AppleLive #scarf #AppleEvent

Now, as great and quick as this parody is – they only tweeted once. This could have been superb.

Tip: Redundant accounts look lazy. If you're going to create a social account, know that it takes graft, and only join if you have time to invest in creating content. If you can't be bothered to tweet, people won't bother following you.

26.
@SteveMartinToGo

Founded: May 2008
Following: 5,343,076

Despite the fact that @SteveMartinToGo is 'currently on a Twitter hiatus', he continues to tweet. So it's less of a hiatus and more of a hi-I'm here.

As in his acting career, Martin is a full-blown funny man on Twitter. His one-liners and ability to turn every 140 characters into a joke has picked him up a substantial following since he joined the social network back in 2008 (he's practically a Twitter veteran).

Here are a few of his best Tweets:

- I have a strange feeling I am being followed
- My wife doesn't know that I'm tweeting. She thinks I'm writing a screenplay
- Had to turn down movie because of Twitter duties. Selling off furniture

Tip: Stick to what you know and your community will follow.

27.
@safiyyahn
Founded: September 2010
Following: 3,785

When @Safiyyahn sent a tweet on New Year's Eve 2013, she probably didn't realise that it would transform her from an average Twitter user (with around 100 followers) into a mini celebrity.

She marvelled that the planet was turning 2,014 years. Now whether this was meant to be funny or she genuinely believed that Earth – which is an estimated 4.54 billion years old – was actually celebrating its 2014th year in existence, the tweet got retweeted over 16,000 times.

She's living proof that, as with most walks of life, some people just strike it really lucky. Though her tweets are pretty throwaway, she continues to rack up a strong following.

Tip: You don't have to be somebody in the real world to be somebody on Twitter.

28.
@MrJamie East
Founded: February 2008
Following: 94,129

What is the favourite button on Twitter actually for? If you're anything like @MrJamieEast, perhaps you'll think 'Twitter should really name the favourite button the "I'm done with this conversation now thanks" button.'

He's a great man to follow for anyone who loves a blunt interpretation of the world.

However, for all his comic brilliance, he's not right about the favourite button. Here are a few ways to get more out of it:

• Read for later: this bookmarks great tweets that you can easily go back to.
• Approval: You like/agree with something.
• Flirting: That subtle acknowledgement that gets people wanting more.
• Awareness: By favouriting you put yourself in front of the tweeter, which could get you a new follower.
• Show your personality: If someone flicks through your favourited tweets, they'll see what you're interested in and what you're about.

With Twitter's new layout (or at least the layout it was using at the time of publishing) your favourited tweets are more visible than ever, which should make you think twice about what it is you want others to see.

Tip: Think about how the favourite button can work for you. Don't favourite lightly.

29.
@LabourPress
Founded: October 2009
Following: 52,029

Did you know, 44% of Twitter accounts have never actually tweeted[2]? People who don't want strangers nicking their name hold a lot of them, while people whose interest in the platform has waned also make up a large percentage. And then, of course, there are those who use the platform as an information highway.

A fantastic example of an account coming under fire for looking as though they've lost interest in Twitter (and its followers) is @LibDemPress.

The Liberal Democrat's press team received a tweet from @LabourPress saying 'Send out the search party - @LibDemPress haven't tweeted since July 13th'. Within seconds, they replied with: 'Sorry, we've been busy running the country. #Coalicious'.

What can you say to that? Labour's joke royally backfired, and proved that politics and social media don't always mix.

Tip: You don't have to tweet but you do have to listen.

---

[2] Twopcharts; a third-party site that monitors Twitter Activity

30.
@KellogsUK
Founded: January 2009
Following: 25,220

Good social practice dictates that brands should aim to deliver customer service across all social platforms, and keep an eye out for opportunities to get involved in some spontaneous fun to bring people closer to that brand.

@KellogsUK did just this. One of its customers found an empty Chewits wrapper in her cereal. She wasn't annoyed; she simply wanted the 'whole' sweet.

She asked if Tony the Tiger could join her for breakfast by way of apology. Soon afterwards, Tony turned up on her doorstep, at which time she tweeted: 'If it weren't for Twitter, Tony the Tiger wouldn't ever have come to my house for tea #twitterbirthday'.

66.7% of all public brand mentions on social media happen on Twitter[3], so if there's a place to respond and act quickly, it's there! For @KellogsUK, this stunt would have cost them very little. But it was a great way to generate brand affection and show they're willing to go above and beyond for their customers.

Tip: Customer service on Twitter is key. It's about being timely and, where possible, going above and beyond to gain your customers' trust.

---

[3] Mention, 2014

31.
@BritneySpears
Founded: September 2008
Following: 39,261,131

iPhone assistants are a thing now. Well, at least they are for celebrities. As essential as an agent or makeup artist, it falls to iPhone assistants to take all those Instagram shots and tweet regular updates – while pretending to be the celeb in question. How else do you think @Rihanna shares those full-length sexy selfies every day, eh?

Sometimes these assistants get it wrong. Really wrong. And @BritneySpears' team is a prime example. There's no attempt to make this account look 'real'. All her messages do is broadcast tour dates with the occasional 'y'all' or emoji tagged on the end. It's dry. And unless Brit has a memory for dates, which is doubtful, the whole account just feels really inauthentic. Here's an example of what I'm saying:

• Ladies in the US & Canada – you don't have to be at #NYFW to see my new line!
Go to intimatebirtneyspears.com to see & shop the collection now!

Twitter is designed to bring you closer to your interests, and this is a less than successful attempt by @BritneySpears' team to do that. If Ms. Spears isn't interested or doesn't have the time, she should be transparent enough to say that her wider team are running the account.

Tip: Appreciate the celebrities out there who take the time to remain genuine. If you get the gig of iPhone assistant, be transparent.

32.
@ThatcherDeadYet

Founded: October 2010
Following: 2,637

When hashtags go wrong, they go *really* wrong.

Prime Minister Margaret Thatcher suffered a fatal stroke in 2013, aged 87. A hugely divisive character in life, her death was equally controversial – not least because of a website dedicated to answering the question 'Is Thatcher Dead Yet?', which later spawned the hashtag #Nowthatchersdead on the day of her passing.

However you felt about her, it's safe to say this website and hashtag weren't exactly an empathetic reaction to the death of an old lady. But worse still, there was a different way to read the hashtag.

With a quick change in capitalisation, it read #NowThatChersDead. This was quickly picked up on Twitter. Was pop megastar and gay icon Cher really dead?

Cher hadn't died (thank GOD), and confirmed this to her 1.4million followers.

Tip: If you're unsure, get a few people to read your hashtag to make sure it can't be misinterpreted.

33.
@ASOS_Menswear
Founded: June 2012
Following: 52,747

@ASOS_Menswear is an excellent Twitter feed. It's timely, topical and always good for a one-liner.

The ASOS Menswear brand is @ASOS' cheeky little brother, and runs its social channels accordingly. It's kind of like the mate you always want to go the pub with, because he's cool, credible and can always be relied on for a laugh.

If you didn't watch this TV show, then you're going to find this next bit weird. When Channel 4 aired a documentary called 'The Man With the Ten Stone Testicles', one of the brand's editors tweeted from @ASOS_Menswear, saying: 'Before you ask, no we will not be ranging scrotum hoodies'. As you can probably imagine, this flew on Twitter, and is the brand's most successful engagement tweet to date. Proof that timely, relevant and funny tweets make the best, most-retweetable content.

Tip: Twitter and TV go hand in hand. Get involved with the conversation happening on Twitter for additional pick up.

34.
@MrsStephenFry

Founded: May 2009
Following: 146,767

If having @StephenFry on Twitter wasn't good enough, perhaps it's time to acquaint you with his 'poor, downtrodden wife & mother of his five, six or possibly even seven kids', Edna Fry.

Ever heard the phrase 'be yourself because everyone else is taken'? Well, on Twitter that's not true. You can be anyone at all – even a parody wife to a national treasure like Fry.

Here are her a few of her best bits:

- Our dog can find anything, it's a Labragoogle.
- Twitter is like a Charles Dickens novel - 140 characters, lots of silly names and it goes on forever.
- In honour of Charlie Chaplin's 122nd birthday, this tweet is silent, black and white and not particularly funny.

@MrsStephenFry hasn't only created an excellent account; she's mocked up an image of what @StephenFry would look like if he were a woman. Even if the tweets weren't up to their scratch (they're always top notch!), just seeing a dragged-up Fry in your feed is sure to bring a smile.

Tip: When setting up your account, consider all the elements that will make you stand out. It's not just the tweets or the name, but really think about your biog – sell yourself, why should people follow you, and what will they get out of your account?

35.
@ArgosHelpers
Founded: June 2010
Following: 11,078

We left 'street' inspired, abbreviated text-speak back in the '90s. In fact, the only person who still uses it is probably your old man, who's just trying to play catch up. Well, him and the @ArgosHelpers, of course.

- @ArgosHelpers YO wen u gettin da ps4 tings in moss side? Ain't waitin no more. Plus da asian guy whu works dere got bare attitude #wasteman
- @BadManBugti Safe badman, we gettin sum more PS4 tings in wivin da next week y'get me. Soz bout da attitude, probz avin a bad day yo.

This conversation was retweeted over 6,000 times, and helped boost the brand's following, while generating a serious amount of positive press.

Tip: Unfortunately, this epic tweet is pretty much a solo experience for Argos. The rest of the time its stream is filled with apologies to disappointed customers. Remember, if you start a tweet with '@', it's only seen by you and people who follow both people tweeting. If you start with anything other than an '@', it goes out to every person that follows you... and that can make you look, in the words of Argos, WELL BAD, BRUV.

36.
@EveryTweet_Ever
Founded: December 2011
Following: 44,043

There is no such thing as an original thought. Or at least, there's rarely an original idea or joke posted on Twitter. However, @EveryTweet_Ever challenges that notion, and prides itself on churning out imaginative, funny tweets.

If you thought that your tweets were unique, it's time to think again. @EveryTweet_Ever plays on the clichéd tweets of the masses, and uses its wit to highlight how moronic they are:

- #FF @ Famous Person Who Already Has Millions of Followers
- #Deliberatelylonghashtagbecausethatisalwaysfunny

Tip: If you want to be unique and stand out, challenge yourself to be different and offer your followers something they can't get elsewhere.

37.
@RobinMcCauley
Founded: July 2009
Following: 50,169

This girl is killing it on Twitter, one tweet at a time. McCauley's unique brand of bitchy deadpan comedy is exactly what this social network was designed for, and an account you absolutely have to follow. In fact, get your phone out this second and do it.

Done it?

Good.

Here are her top 5 most 'retweetable' Twitter jokes/reasons to follow:

- Saw a couple holding hands while jogging and it made me hopeful that one day I will meet someone who will hate them with me.
- A woman started choking in the line at Starbucks- it was so scary but thankfully someone opened another register.
- I hate it when I think I'm buying ORGANIC vegetables but when I get home I discover they're just REGULAR donuts.
- Being an adult is 99% wondering how you hurt your back.
- A fun thing to do at parties is stay home and watch TV.

Tip: Say things in a novel way and you'll have no problem with standing out on Twitter.

38.
@Johnjannuzzi

Founded: March 2009
Following: 34,244

@Johnjannuzzi is @GQ's Senior Digital Editor. He uses Twitter to report the peculiarities of working in fashion, while poking fun at the more mundane aspects of the industry. Think The Devil Wears Prada, but realistic and with more charisma.

From work breaks at @Starbucks to his love/hate relationship with Mean Girls, he gives his followers a front row seat to a day in the life of Jannuzzi. And although it's not the wall-to-wall glamour one might expect, it's a great insight into what a career in topflight journalism is truly like.

Here is a snippet of what to expect:

- The one thing I hate about the Ice Cream man is he expects me to pay for ice cream.
- You made me sprint over here. What more do you want?
- Do you think Malia Obama is ever like, "Dad, I cannot with this right now." and then he's like "Yes we can."?

Tip: Bring people closer to your world and they'll engage with you.

39.
@USASoccerGuy
Founded: March 2013
Following: 365,941

Although some people fail to recognise it, this, right here, is a spoof account. @USASoccerGuy plays on the belief that Americans just don't get the concept or appeal of British football. He does this by positioning himself as a (fake) soccer pundit, who has a questionable knowledge of the beautiful game.

He live tweets matches and offers a hilarious blow-by-blow commentary, littered with Americanisms that are at odds with socially accepted footie language. For instance, every time a goal is scored, he tweets 'GOALSHOT'.

@USASoccerGuy has also created a line of t-shirts, including slogan tees that read 'Aston Vanilla' or 'Knotting-ham Tree Huggers'. Priceless.

But it's his replies that make this account worth following...

• This soccer match just shows that without Santiago Munez, New Castle are not a threat. #BringSantiagoBack
• Barcelonia heading for Soccertime sadness in the Lana Del Ray soccer cup. #realsaltlakemadrid
• GOOOOOOOOOOOOOOOOAAAAAAAAAAALLLLLLLLSS SSSHHHHHHOOOOOOOTTTTTTTTTTAGAHAHAHSHAJE KFKDOWJDJSIWBDJSUWJDJDJ!!!!

Tip: Two way conversation, all the way. It's good to talk, so keep replying to people who take the time to respond to your tweets.

40.
@Budlight
Founded: August 2012
Following: 110,195

Using words to communicate is, like, super boring. That's why emojis – the first universal language – are all the rage.

With emojis, you have it all – facial expressions, loved up cats, and more pictorial wonderfulness besides. You can harness the communicative power of the emoji to say literally anything (*inserts bell emoji and the word 'end' here).

@Budlight is a corking example of this; many of its tweets are carefully crafted exclusively from emojis and a relevant hashtags. For example, take a look at the brand's #4thofJuly post below:

#4thofJuly

Tip: Keep it simple. Keep it visual. Keep it relevant and you'll keep growing on Twitter.

41.
@WillColey
Founded: March 2008
Following: 5,271

Used properly, a hashtag is a great way of contributing towards trending topics and improves the visibility of your tweet. They're also a nice way of injecting some humour into your tweets when used sparingly.

However, there are few things more infuriating than someone who gets hashtag happy. And this overuse is something @WillColey likes to get really #vocal about on Twitter.

While hashtags are useful and streamline a conversation, if that's all you use in your tweets they become unreadable and, well, desperate.

Tip: Hashtags are super important and really help to gain exposure, but limit it to things that are relevant. One or two will cut it.

42.
@HumbleBrag
Founded: November 2010
Following: 252,682

No one wants to share a picture of themselves in pyjamas, eating Ben & Jerry's out of the tub on a Sunday... but if you happen to supping champagne somewhere fabulous, you sure as hell want to let everyone know about it. And social media provides the perfect outlet for that.

Put simply, people use Twitter to show off. #Fact.

@HumbleBrag, an account run by Parks & Recreation writer Harris Whittle, takes those people DOWN. Whether you're a celeb or just a fellow average Joe, be careful flaunting it on Twitter, because this account is out to get you. It hunts down the boastful and publically shames them.

This account has even got 'HumbleBrag' into the Urban Dictionary, which defines it as follows: 'Subtly letting others now about how fantastic your life is while undercutting it with a bit of self-effacing humor or "woe is me" gloss.

Uggggh just ate about fifteen piece of chocolate gotta learn to control myself when flying first class or they'll cancel my modelling contract LOL :p #humblebrag"

Tip: Try not too brag too much. Making it onto this feed isn't really a compliment.

43.
@JoshGondelman
Founded: August 2009
Following: 39,737

The majority of people on Twitter use it to waste time while queuing, waiting at the bar, sitting on the lav, or commuting to work. So it's no wonder the brands that recognise this, and respond with great escapist content, have become juggernauts on Twitter (think @RedBull and @Oreo, for instance).

There are individuals out there who are ace at the whole time-wasting thing, too. @JoshGondelman has marked himself out as the man to follow for killer one-liners and answers to questions no one asked. He's the kind of guy you'd want to get caught down the pub with for a lock in. But in case that never happens, settle for following him on Twitter, and it's *almost* like you're in the pub with him.

Here's a handpicked selection of his best musings on life:

- HOW HAS THERE NOT BEEN A GPS CALLED THE GARMIN SANDIEGO?
- If you want to rob a white person, just say: "Stop, collaborate, and listen," then steal their stuff while they rap the rest of the song
- I bet Duck Tales was going to be called Duck Stories, and then one guy was like: "Are you ready for me to blow your mind?"

Tip: Create content that'll help you to really stand out on a social channel where there's already a lot of noise.

44.
@Sarcastialist
Founded: December 2013
Following: 15,367

Scott Schuman's The Sartorialist is the toast of the fashion industry. He travels the world, taking pictures of inspirational street style looks, and shares them on his blog, Twitter and Instagram.

The @Sacastialist, on the other hand, is a spoof account that makes a mockery of these same photos. It's a spoof account with a difference, though. Rather than having the troll-like tone shared by most of these kinds of accounts have, his is more playful and gently mocking - his tweets feel genuinely endearing, rather than cruel or nasty.

There's too many good ones, I couldn't choose my favourite so put the book down and go check out his snaps on Twitter.

Tip: Pictures and humour go hand in hand. Make it bespoke and tailored to you, then you'll have no problem smashing those engagement targets.

45.
@HMVTweets
Founded: November 2008
Following: 94,854

If you're a company making major redundancies, make sure to change your social passwords before you piss your (soon to be former) employees off. This is a lesson HMV learnt the hard way.

HMV's past Social Media Planner felt like @HMVTweets never really took social media seriously and failed to harness its power – something, which, in his opinion, lead to the brand's eventual undoing.

Unfortunately for the onetime high street favourite, Twitter was a great way for one former employee to get her point across, and quickly.

Here is an example:

• Just overheard our Marketing Director (he's staying, folks!) ask "How do I shut down Twitter?" #HMVXFactorFiring

The live tweets to HMV's lay offs were timely, newsy, and, as such, the press pick up was, as you might expect, explosive.

Tip: Keep a close eye on who has access to your social channels, and regularity update the passwords. Call it, covering your back.

46.
@KennethCole
Founded: May 2012
Following: 140,591

If you're a major brand, there's never a good time to tweet about politics. Apparently designer @KennethCole never received that memo. Worse still he tweeted about politics in order to piggyback a trending hashtag.

When the Egyptian Revolution of 2011 gathered pace, people tweeted in their thousands in support of the uprising, using #Cairo. Including @KennethCole...

This is what he said: 'Millions are in uproar in #Cairo. Rumor is they heard our new spring collection is available now'. Understandably, this tweet resulted in a massive online backlash, and demanded Cole make a public apology which read: 'I've dedicated my life to raising awareness about serious social issues, and in hindsight my attempt at humor regarding a nation liberating themselves against oppression was poorly timed and absolutely inappropriate.'

And yet, in 2013, he did it again. This time, he quipped about U.S. military intervention in Syria.

So, why keep doing it? Cole says these gaffes are good for business. In an interview with @HuffingtonPost he said: 'Our stock went up that day, and I picked up 3,000 new followers on Twitter.'

Tip: Needless to say, if you want to build a loyal following of valuable customers who trust you (and want to buy your gear), this probably isn't the strongest social strategy to roll out.

47.
@JakeFogelnest
Founded: April 2008
Following: 74,618

The increasing use of dual-screening (using your smartphone while watching TV) has given rise to loads of great marketing campaigns. It also allows mischief-makers, like comedian, writer, and all-round Twitter pro @JakeFogelnest to have some fun with audiences by tweeting along to films and television shows.

Foglenest had fans of Martin Scorsese's Goodfellas eating out of the palm of his hand when he set up an account that, randomly, celebrated the 34th anniversary of Henry Hill's arrest – one of the movie's lead characters, played by Ray Liotta. He set up @SundayMay11th and tweeted from it as though he was Hill.

Here are few of his expertly crafted tweets, which made it seem as though these (fictitious) events were happening in real time.

- Gotta drop off some guns at Jimmy's to match some silencers he has. They're great guns, he's gonna be real happy.
- Jimmy says the drugs are turning my mind into mush. :(
- Helicopter is back. Karen saw it. #FML

This was a great way to pay homage to a fantastic film, and make jokes that appeal to its loyal fan base.

Tip: If there's something relevant on TV – live tweet, join that conversation using the relevant hashtag.

140 ULTIMATE TWITTER LOLS

3.
General LOLs

Cut a fat slice of funny pie and tuck into these hilarious Twitter handles.

48.
@PharrellHat

Founded: June 2014
Following: 19,799

Is it funny or depressing to think we live in a world where a hat has its own Twitter account? Either way, it does.

But this isn't just any hat, of course.

This is the @VivienneWestwood headpiece that @Pharrell wore to the 2014 Grammy Awards.

Within minutes of his arrival on the red carpet, Pharrell's hat went viral. As with all social media successes, someone acted at lightening speed to set up its own parody Twitter account, which, by the end of the evening, boasted over 19,000 followers. The account was picked up by a plethora of media outlets, including GQ and The Today Show, and is testament to the power of reactive behaviour on social.

Tip: Speed.

49.
@HonestToddler
Founded: May 2012
Following: 295,717

Some Twitter accounts score high on the LOL-scale because of their ability to signpost humour in things you hadn't noticed were funny before.

@HonestToddler does just that. This account speaks as though a toddler could articulate the absurdity of their circumstances the way adults can. For instance, they might say funny things like:

- If you did a secret poo on the floor, would you bring mommy to it, cover it with a blanket, or hide? Asking for a friend.
- Crushed the contents of an entire box of Ritz crackers. Hungry for Ritz crackers. Not these ones. They're broken.
- Back tapping. Don't try to rush it. Don't lean on my crib either. Use your core.

Tip: Twitter allows people and objects that don't have a voice, to have a voice.

50.
@Pundamentalism

Founded: December 2010
Following: 55,089

It sounds simple, mostly because it is, but James Martin's Twitter account (a.k.a. @Pundamentalism) built its reputation on pumping out puns. And, let me tell you, they're bloody good.

Here are a few of my faves:

- "Great British Bake-Off tonight. In honor of the iPhone launch last night, they too will be trying to improve the Apple Turnover."
- "Dear whoever stole my copy of Microsoft Office - I will track you down. You have my Word."
- "My mate's addicted to helium balloons. He speaks very highly of them."

Twitter is chock-full of funny people. However, accounts that publish the kind of genuine LOLs that you would happily share with your old man without blushing are few and far between. @Pundamentalism is good, clean fun, and Twitter word play at its best.

Like a true social media pro, he's built a reputation on tapping into real-time moments and spinning an awesome tweet out of them. Essentially, he's here to make your life easier. You don't need to stress it – you just need to retweet and share his gag as if it were your own. @ExcuseThePun is also worth checking out!

Tip: Think real-time, think dual screen.

51.
@__MichaelJOrdan
Founded: March 2012
Following: 40,667

First thing's first: considering the number of parody accounts with huge followings out there, it's ridiculous that this account hasn't blown up in the same way. It's currently at a mere 40K followers, yet it's easily one of the best out there.

It's completely nuts, but because of the seamlessly integrated references to Jordan's sporting and film career, it also feels pretty authentic. And that's what makes it so damn good!

Here are a few of the parody slam-dunker's best tweets:

- At my funeral I want to be dunked into my casket
- Some guy got my phone number and keeps texting "Remember Space Jam?". I don't need this.
- i only agreed to go salsa dancing because i thought it was going to be a tasty experience, well it wasn't
- I was just thinking: cats don't have butt cheeks

Tip: Nostalgia always works on social!

52.
@Darth
Founded: March 2007
Following: 27,115

@Darth – no, not he of Star Wars fame – but in actual fact, a helmet-wearing Red Panda is next up. Whoever's behind this account keeps a low profile, but if ever he reveals himself, there will be people lining up to congratulate him on his epic Photoshop skills.

Check out some of his most LOL-inducing stuff over on Twitter and follow @Darth's hilarious updates in real time.

Now, the one strange thing about this Twitter account is the fact that they occasionally delete their tweets so, if you like what you see, save it now or it may be gone forever.

Tip: Don't be quick to delete, even if you've made an error – the way that you handle that typo or mistake can make you look human, which helps. Obviously, if it's a big boo-boo then delete and apologise.

53 & 54.
@PaulChuckle2 @BazElliot

Founded: November 2012 / June 2012
Following: 59,734 / 49,174

Everyone loves a bit of nostalgia, and nothing resonates with a 90s child quite like The Chuckle Brothers.

It was only a matter of time before this duo joined the Twittersphere and filled people's feeds with, inexplicably, lots of Rotherham United updates and selfies. And unlike many comedians on Twitter, these guys take the time to reply to their fans, ensuring everyone takes a trip down memory lane and enjoys some nostalgia-fuelled LOLs.

They've got separate accounts and, if you ask nicely, they'll even give you a cheeky retweet or two.

Tip: Reply to your followers; it's always great exposure and makes them feel valued.

55 & 56.
@PreSchoolGems @HighgateMums

Founded: April 2010 / May 2012
Following: 202,239 / 12,691

As the saying goes 'kids say the funniest things', which is why this account has earned its spot in #TwitterLOLs. The idea isn't new; reporting the funny things kids say in complete innocence is something parents around the globe have done for ages. But sharing it on Twitter is novel outlet, which helps keep the concept fresh.

A preschool teacher who shares all the delightful titbits that she overhears from her students curates this feed. It's touching, strange and always good for a laugh. Here are a few of the best bits:

- "I have crazy stuff going on in my mind. I can dream about brownies even as I am eating them."
- "I'm mad at my imaginary friend. I told her not to get another job, but she snuck out and found a new one."
- "My mom is going to pick me up from school today and she does not have a penis."

Now, if you're a fan of the random crap that comes out of kids' mouths, then check out @Highgatemums, too. These two accounts aren't connected, but both deserved a mention. Highgate – an affluent area in North London – is a place where the mums are almost as bad (for all the wrong reasons) as their kids. Here are a few snippets that will give you a teaser of the account:

- 'I throw my arms up and thank God for the iPad. Although the au pair keeps using it to talk to her family, wherever they are.'
- 'We're begging for her to be let off school Monday and Tuesday. She gets terrible jetlag even from Europe.'
- 'On a rainy day like this do people really think kids should go to school on public transport. Really?'

Tip: Use Twitter as a live ticker to something that's going on in or around your life, thinks of it as a live journal (without the waffle!).

57.
@HappyBirthTime
Founded: March 2014
Following: 11,421

What do you get when you mix a celebrity's birthday, another celebrity's quote, and a completely random picture? Say hello to @HappyBirthTime.

If you're wondering what the point of this account is, then it's done its job. Like most Internet phenomena, there's no real rhyme or reason behind it – it's totally bizarre. And it works.

Whatever idea you have, however weird, Twitter is ready for you. And the stranger and more obscure you can make it, the better. Unleashing weird on the world is a great way to gain followers... but not necessarily the most normal ones.

Tip: With 500million tweets sent per day[4], you have to do something to stand out. So head into the Twittersphere and get random.

---

[4] Twitter Inc. 2014

58.
@whitegrlproblem
Founded: March 2010
Following: 811,962

@Whitegrlproblem AKA Babe Walker has her social media game nailed: she has in excess of 800k followers on Twitter and over 260k on Facebook. And there's a reason for that: the 'grl' is funny.

In 140 characters, she shares acutely observed, satirical commentary on the world of a twenty-something, middle-class white girl, who has a less than robust understanding of racial or gender politics. She endorses the ignorant stereotype everyone loves to hate; but Walker's tongue sits firmly in her cheek, so the thoughts she expresses through @Whitegrlproblem are always humorous and, to a degree, darkly relatable.

Here are 5 issues that you probably share with @Whitegrlproblem, but that you would never, ever say out loud:

- I'm crying into a salad.
- I believe in hate at first sight.
- I love watching couples fight. Love it. Love it so much.
- Sorry I forgot to text you for a year.
- No, you don't get it. I want you to hate me.

Tip: If you want people to engage with you, they need to be able to relate to you.

59.
@Jesus_M_Christ
Founded: April 2009
Following: 457,771

Before a brand or individual kicks off their social strategy, identifying the right audience is key.

For @Jesus_M_Christ, it was easy. He addresses everyone – after all, this parody account is God's representative ~~on Earth~~ online.

If profanity is your thing, check out some of his best bad taste tweets below.

- Whoa, Chick-Fil-A. Just because I said I liked your chicken sandwich, doesn't mean I endorse your views on marriage
- BREAKING NEWS from Rebecca Black: Tomorrow is Saturday and Sunday comes afterwards.
- Sorry about the hurricane everyone. But if you continue to make episodes of Jersey Shore this is going to keep happening.

We've got a good balance here. It's not just about proactively tweeting, @Jesus_M_Christ replies and favourites tweets, and posts his own content. A nice, eclectic account, JMC.

Tip: Use all of Twitter's features – don't just tweet; favourite, reply and retweet to maximise opportunity.

60.
@KimKierkegaard

Founded: June 2012
Following: 148,516

If, like me, you're a member of the anti-Kardashian committee, you're sure to love @KimKierkegaard.

Not that Mrs Kanye West really needs a parody account (surely she's become a parody of herself by now), but this spoof profile has been done brilliantly.

@KimKierkegaard lampoons the frivolous content of Kim Kardashian's tweets, passing them through the lens of tormented Danish philosopher Soren Kierkegaard. The result? Tweets that compare deviating from a diet plan with the futility of existence. Like, totally deep.

Here are a few of my favourites:

- Rise & grind! Busy day!! Gym then packing 4 Paris again! This is the despair of finitude, when the self is lost to the temporal, the trivial
- No filter. No photoshop. The highest and most beautiful things are not to read about or seen, but to be lived. Summertime yoga.
- Just go the best spray tan!!!! There is an indescribable joy that glows through us unaccountably.

Tip: If you're out to create a parody, the lesson here is to take the character and really exaggerate them. Just like this one sends up how mundane Kimmy K's tweets are.

61.
@Wordstigram
Founded: June 2012
Following: 228,053

Now this is genius.

In 140 characters, the person behind this account sums up what's happening in people's Instagram pictures. Each tweet captures an Insta-cliché perfectly and, as such, they are instantly relatable – everyone has that person in his or her feed.

Here are a just a few examples of when @Wordstigram has hit the nail squarely on the head:

- Two girls who look nothing like each other, caption: "Sooo happy to have my twin back."
- Screenshot of a conversation that makes no sense to anyone and the caption reads "Omggg this is why I love her #BffProbs"
- A picture of a Polaroid with two girls dressed the same making peace signs at a music festival. Caption: "Ugh take me back"

Fun, light-hearted and oh-so-of-the-moment, @Wordstigram does all the bitching for you.

Tip: Can't find the time to tweet? Put a few minutes aside each morning and schedule tweets throughout the day.

62.
@MayorOfLondon
Founded: May 2008
Following: 1,030,000

The Mayor of London ran a Twitter Q&A called #AskBoris. Known for his floppy hair, affable demeanour and general buffoonery, broadly speaking, Boris is quite well liked... for a politician.

But if you had access to the Mayor, what would you ask him?

Here's what a few oddballs wanted to know:

- Can I crash at your place til I find a place to live in London?
- Boris, please can you get the buses to play the Thunderbirds theme music when the disabled ramp is deployed? #AskBoris
- If you ever went bald would you consider wearing a toupee? #allyourpowerisinyourhair #AskBoris

Boris did his best to ignore the more surreal tweets. But as the session was marketed as an 'ask-me-anything' session, what else could he expect?

Next time, Bo-Jo, outline a more specific framework of questioning, otherwise you'll just have a repeat performance.

Tip: Think about what you'd like to get out of social media. Message things in a way that narrows down the options.

63.
@Lord_Voldemort7
Founded: May 2011
Following: 1,376

It's been three years since the last Harry Potter film was released, but this fictional account for Lord Voldemort helps keep the Harry Potter magic alive.

If you're a Pot head, there are plenty of references to Harry, Hermione and co. to keep you entertained. The great thing about this account, though, is how these references are given a timely spin, and comment on newsy bites and pop culture.

Here are a few examples:

- So I'm assuming that North West won't be a One Direction fan?
- If you don't get my Harry Potter references then there is something Siriusly Ron with you.
- #ReasonsWhyIHateSchool: It's not Hogwarts

Tip: Look at what's trending on Twitter and create tweets that are relevant to you around the trending topics and hashtags.

64.
@IvyBean104
Founded: May 2009
Following: 37,959

Although Ivy Bean passed away in 2010, she did so, aged 104, having claimed the title of oldest active Twitter user in the world.

Who said the digital revolution was for members of Generation Y or younger, eh?

Nowadays, half the population is under the age of 30, and has never really experienced life without the Internet. Yes, this is a #fact.

Twitter is a sadder place without Ivy. Imagine how much nicer the social space would be with more old ladies in it. More people would feel inclined to mind their manners for one thing!

Tip: Don't be naive enough to think that social is only for the young. Even if you're targeting an older demographic – they also might be on Twitter.

Here is something you might not have known, grandparents are the fastest growing demographic on Twitter.[5]

---

[5] Erik Quelman - NEW FACT

65.
@JohnCMayerMusic
Founded: June 2009
Following: 1,657

Twitter is obviously a great way to instantly let people know what you are doing but it's also a great way to instantly kill yourself. When you're an idiot, people learn that you're an idiot instantly.

Twitter is a great way to gain exposure and build your online profile quickly. Unfortunately for some, however, it's also where you can damage the reputation you've fought so hard for quicker than the time it takes to say 'LOL!'.

This something serial womaniser and crooner @JohnCMayber knows only too well. Not so long ago, he tweeted the following, and his cool factor was ruined forever:

'BREAKING CELEBRITY NEWS: I was sitting with my legs crossed for far too long and my penis fell asleep.'

Tip: One tweet, that's all it takes!

66.
@BollocksWeather
Founded: December 2013
Following: 28,890

The bio says it all: 'The Fucking Weather, told how it is. Fuck all to do with the Met Office. And more accurate.'

Britain is a nation obsessed by the weather. Whether it's hot, cold, wet or dry, people love complaining about it on Twitter. @BollocksWeather taps into that behaviour, and gives its followers an outlet for their meteorological frustrations.

Cleverly, it also uses relevant trending hashtags to boost awareness; for instance, the time it updated its followers on the weather in the form of a poem to celebrate #NationalPoetsDay, entitled 'Today's Fucking Weather':

The sun is out,
The sky is blue,
Boring as fuck really
Just like you.
@b0ringtweets
#NationalPoetryDay

Tip: Each time you're on Twitter, look at what's trending and see whether there's a hook for your feed. This is great for additional awareness and keeping your feed topical.

67.
@GayCode
Founded: September 2011
Following: 2,191

It's time to fine-tune your gaydar.

Like the late @Joan_Rivers, this account sees the innuendo and double entendre in everything.

Simply by adding 'Gay Code' at the start of tweets it finds around Twitter, it turns seemingly innocuous statements and questions into subtle homoeroticisms. And the effect is really funny.

Next time you tweet something, think if it could be misconstrued as 'Gay Code' first. And if it can, cross your fingers @GayCode picks it up, and turns you into a Twitter celeb for 15 minutes.

Tip: Measure the success of your Twitter account not by the following, but by the engagement levels that you see on each tweet.

68.
@TinderLikeBrent
Founded: June 2014
Following: 18,514

WARNING: This account contains themes of an adult nature.

Fans of @RickyGervais' sitcom The Office should need no reminder of its cringeworthy protagonist, David Brent.

This account challenges its followers to secure a date on Tinder using classic, squirm-inducing Brentisms, and later share the conversations on Twitter.

As you might imagine, the results aren't always   successful, but they're always funny. Below is an example of one man's attempt to score using Brent quotes.

- 'Ha ha I think your just winding me up...But why.
- 'No no I'm not - it was for you to fill in! To what extent do YOU believe you have the skills and knowledge to perform your job effectively?
- Hmm not sure, the company has doubled it's turnover since i've started so I must be making a difference. In your personal opinion what's the difference between Jam and Marmalade?
- But what's the single most important thing for a company? Is it the turnover? Is it the stock? It's the people.

Tip: Tinder is bang on trend right now, for one of these immediate hit-Twitter accounts. Look at what topics and accounts have a high share of voice on Twitter and put a spin on it.

69.
@AxTang
Founded: July 2008
Following: 12,334

Humour is a very subjective thing. And if you're looking for funny-ha-ha, this account probably isn't for you. But for those of you with a darker sense of humour, @AxTang should be right up your street.

@AxTang is a real pick me up account, mainly because he makes his followers thankful the things he tweets about are happening to him, not them.

Here is what to expect:

- *wakes up in a cold sweat* what the fuck is up with boat shoes
- I'm just a sophisticated dude with a lot of nice sweaters looking to have a good time on the web
- I love when women can be straightforward about what they want. like, "i want to murder you," or "i'm going to murder you."

Simplicity at its finest.

Tip: You gotta be real on Twitter. Mundane is one thing but keep what you're eating or the weather updates to a minimum.

70.
@IllustratedTypo
Founded: September 2013
Following: 5,810

Twitter is full of typos. It's all about getting things out quickly and being first, so sometimes there's no time to check your spelling, grammar and punctuation. Or at least that's the excuse.

@IllustratedTypo goes on the hunt for offending accounts that make the very best of the worst typos and grammatical errors, and turns them into pictures. 'iFawn' rather than 'iPhone' – you can imagine the image already, can't you?

Like this? Check out @AnimatedTweet.

Tip: Tweets with pictures help to drive interaction and engagement; those tweets stand out more than those when you're passively reading and, if you're anything like @IllustratedTypo, you won't think twice about sharing with your followers.

71.
@NightClubFails

Founded: April 2012
Following: 411,856

That feeling when you wake up after a heavy night out, check your phone, and see a push notification that reads 'Tagged in a picture'. Your heart sinks and you ready yourself for the worst photo of you ever taken. Yup, that feeling.

Well, imagine if your picture ended up on @NightClubFails, and you (yes, YOU!) become an overnight Internet hit.

The goal of this account is quite simple: embarrass the hell out of someone, while making everyone thankful it's not them. The people behind this account own none of the pictures - they simply curate the very best (and shameful) pics floating around the net, and feature them on their feed.

This is targeted at those who love to party, and want to wake up on a Sunday feeling grateful things didn't get that out of hand.

Tip: Drink in moderation and know your audience. Once you know who you're talking to, you can create a constant stream of updates that will get them every time.

Oh, and never tweet under the influence, obvs!

72.
@rare_basement
Founded: April 2009
Following: 44,811

If eccentric, oddball humour is your thing, get an eyeful of @rare_basement's Twitter feed. Follow and join her community of peculiarity and last.fm obsessives.

With tweets like these, it's no wonder she's became a shining light in the subculture of online comedy:

- 'im pretty popular on the internet,' i whisper to my cat. cat doesnt respond because cat doesnt exist. there is no cat and i am alone
- i was making fun of the cat by imitating her and i pulled a muscle in my neck so she got the last laugh
- if u could kiss one dog on the mouth which dog would it be. dont reply with ur answer or say it out loud. just think about it for a while

@WeirdHorse and @Egg_Dog are also weird and wonderful animal related accounts worth checking out.

Tip: If there's an animal involved, the Internet is sold on it!

73.
@SexyExecutive

Founded: June 2009
Following: 7,640

Big companies make a habit of getting on people's tits (including mine). That's why @SexyExecutive works – because it takes banal workplace chat and goings on, filters them through the eyes of an office worker with a wicked, irreverent sense of humour, and turns them into something funny and shareable.

Anyone who's ever experienced a day's office work can relate to tweets like:

- Doing a bit of printer-sitting for John Denslow. I pop round and run off a few sheets every night to stop the toner settling.
- Not that I ever do any rubbing out. The eraser is an emotional crutch for the weak and indecisive.
- I have been asked to apologise for appearing to endorse holding your breath while going to the toilet.

Sure, this account is 100% pointless. But thanks to @SexyExecutive's mind-reading capabilities, it makes for a great follow. When you're on your next fag break at work, scrolling through your Twitter feed and see one of its brilliant tweets, you'll no doubt be able to relate to the painfully accurate observations it makes about colleagues and water cooler 'banter'.

Tip: Be relatable.

74.
@ZoeLondonDJ
Founded: July 2010
Following: 23,818

The internet isn't all cat memes, GIFs, porn, and viral videos - it's also the breeding ground for an ever-growing population of bloggers and vloggers. With their numbers on the rise, it's become increasingly difficult to stand out. But there's one who really shines (not least because of her luminous head of dyed hair). Meet Zoe - a.k.a. @ZoeLondonDJ.

First off, she's a @Metallica tee collector, which marks her out as pretty cool (obviously). But she's also brilliant at communicating with her audience and has perfected ways of showing off her personality - something which is really hard to do on Twitter. She tweets little and often, providing her followers with short, snappy updates on what she's up to. This obviously narrows the distance between her and the people looking at her feed, and because she's always doing cool stuff, she reminds people why they follower her - which is to live vicariously through her!

She knows what she likes and how to appeal to a wide audience, and that's why she's racking up those followers.

Tip: Be a personality else you'll blend into the background.

75.
@SoVeryBritish
Founded: December 2012
Following: 872,965

If you're socially awkward and relish the misfortune of others, two things are near certain: first, you're British. Second, you will love this Twitter account. @SoVeryBritish is uproariously entertaining and instantly shareable, because it playfully taps into all sorts of British stereotypes.

Let's mix this up a bit. Take the quiz below and see which of @SoVeryBritish's tweets you've thought at some stage:

[ ] "Fancy a quick half?" - Translation: Fancy going into this pub for as long as possible?

[ ] Being more excited to have an airport beer at 7am than you are about any other part of your holiday

[ ] Not wanting to use an emoticon but worrying that you'll come across as sarcastic without one

[ ] Seeing someone you know walking just ahead of you, so stopping dead in the street until they are completely out of sight.

[ ] Noticing a small patch of blue sky and immediately purchasing 24 cases of Pimms.

Congrats, you scored 5/5. Now you understand why this Twitter account is so on the money.

Tip: Tap into people's mindsets, get them thinking 'Wait, I was just wondering/doing that!'

76.
@tbhplzstop
Founded: March 2012
Following: 163,414

This account is like reading your thoughts in tweet form. Sarcastic and to the point, @tbhplzstop offers a master class in snappy tweets that tap into the mindset of the average teen or twenty-something girl.

Just check these tweets, and you'll get it:

• Kinda wanna look good in a bikini kinda wanna eat three burritos from chipotle kinda pissed i have to pick one.
• I text back embarrassingly fast or three hours later there is no in between.
• Wait a minute this isn't my homework. This is twitter. How did this happen.
• Jealous of girls who wear their hair up and still look female
• if your snapchat story is 200 seconds or more u better be skydiving &doing back flips w Jesus bc trust me your life is not that interesting.

It's as though this account raided your latest Whatsapp conversation with your best friend and broadcast it online. It's totally shareable, which is probably why it's got such a strong following.

Tip: Don't overthink it!

77.
@_YouHadOneJob
Founded: August 2013
Following: 262,821

YOU HAD ONE JOB!!!

Thank goodness! Someone finally set up an account dedicated to celebrating the incompetence of people who have the simplest of tasks to complete and, yet, for whatever reason, fail to do them properly.

From mimes on the streets that have been out-mimed by passersby, to typos in newspapers, @_YouHadOneJob brings everyday blunders to the forefront of the Twitter consciousness, and provides LOLs by the bucketload.

Tip: The Internet is a place for collaboration; Twitter allows us to connect with almost anyone, with just about any hobby going.

78.
@GooglyEyes
Founded: August 2012
Following: 106,000

Fact: people want retweets. That's how to get your name out there and keep follower numbers creeping in the right direction.

@GooglyEyes, an account that believes 'everything is better with eyes', has super strong retweet game.

Whether it's a truck, a house or some scrapped material – they see faces everywhere! They post images and add captions to help you identify the face in everyday objects.

Tip: As you, the follower, can also see the face – you instantly want to Retweet it. So, how do you get the perfect Retweet, if you don't see eyes in everything?

• Aim for 120 characters. This leaves space for the name of the retweeter and doesn't cut off what you have to say.
• Always leave the credit of who you retweeted; it's Twitter etiquette don't ya know!
• Don't be afraid to ask for a retweet, if you think something is valuable. Just be polite.

If you're interested in this one, also check out @Facespics.

79.
@NYC_Blonde
Founded: July 2011
Following: 89,170

Everyone has thoughts they know can never be expressed out loud. That is, of course, unless you do so anonymously. And where's the easiest place to shoot your mouth off and protect you anonymity? Twitter.

@NYC_Blonde is a blogger whose identity is a fiercely guarded secret. She (or perhaps he – who knows!) has built her reputation on saying exactly what other people want to, but don't. She's ballsy, sarcastic and 100% self-indulgent – just the way people on Twitter like it. And her unapologetic, no holds barred approach makes this account hugely retweetable and engaging.

Following @NYC_Blonde allows you to see New York life through a totally fabulous lens.

Tip: Use lists grouped by sectors or topics to follow people you're interested in.

80.
@Queen_UK
Founded: May 2010
Following: 1,189,386

Unlike Queen Elizabeth II, the @Queen_UK only came to her Twitter throne in 2010. At the time, the Telegraph proclaimed that Her Majesty the Queen had 'taken a bold step by becoming the first member of the royal family to join Twitter.' Just to clarify, this is, of course, a parody account.

Despite the fact that this spoof profile is one of the first of its kind, it's a great example of how, done properly, send ups like this one can remain fresh and funny.

This account gives an insight into the (imagined) world of Her Maj. If you've ever struggled to envisage Liz hanging out at Buckingham Palace, sinking an ice-cold gin and tonic, while catching up on the latest episode of Corrie, then this paints the picture with hilarious clarity.

Light-hearted and endearing, @Queen_UK kicks out more LOL moments than you can shake a diamond-encrusted sceptre at. So, get following for real-time, gin-soaked views on current affairs, and there'll be a smile on your face with every tweet. Oh, and her life motto is one seriously worth remembering at times of stress: 'Sod it!'

Tip: In order to get big, you need to nail your tone of voice which is where this account excels.

81.
@TrekAmerica

Founded: November 2009
Following: 4,540

Some things can only happen on Twitter. And #GiveGregTheHoliday was one of them.

For those of you who missed it, Greg Heaslip, a security guard at retail giant The Arcadia Group, accidentally sent a holiday request to the entire company. Now this would be considered a cock up at any office, but at somewhere as big as Arcadia, it's a shambles. His pals quickly to took to Twitter, spreading word of his misfortune and laughing at his expense.

Then the office opposite The Arcadia Group put up a sign saying #GiveGregTheHoliday. A catchy hashtag that went viral in minutes.

A social high five to @TrekAmerica who jumped on the trending topic and offered to send Greg to Vegas, all expenses paid: 'We're taking action and have decided to #givegregtheholiday. A TrekAmerica mini adventure with flights to Vegas. #GregGotTheHoliday!'

@TrekAmerica was quick off the mark, and kept its content relevant and, most importantly, offered a money-can't-buy trip. Its actions had a knock on effect, which got brands all over the world wanting a slice of the conversation. Clothes, books, insurance for his holiday – you name it, he was getting it free.

There were brands that weren't a natural fit trying to get involved, but their offers and input into the conversation fell flat.

Tip: Only get involved in the wider conversation if you actually have a reason to be there!

In case you were wondering how Greg got on in Vegas, he donated everything he received to charity. Naww, we like Greg!

82.
@BruceAtWedding
Founded: August 2014
Following: 21,526

Worship at the altar of Hull City manager Steve Bruce.

This parody account has a cult following, and features images of his infamous pitch-side pose photoshopped into wedding snaps. Completely normal.

Whether it's a Royal Wedding or your mate's party, one thing's for sure – Bruce was there. These images are spreading across Twitter in their hundreds – just search the hashtag #SteveBruceAtWeddings and take a look.

Sure, It's just a bit of fun, but this account is fast becoming a favourite on the Twitter lists. And it's doing great things to upend Steve Bruce's dull reputation.

If you like this account, also check out @Odd_Miliband. You won't be disappointed.

Tip: It pays to be positive and funny on Twitter.

83.
@HilariousSelfies
Founded: ACCOUNT SUSPENDED
Following: ACCOUNT SUSPENDED

Everyone's guilty of having taken a selfie at one time or another (or, if you're @KimKarshashian, several times a day). And this account, as one might expect, does exactly what it says on the tin by curating the best, most hilarious selfies found on Twitter and Instagram.

If your selfie makes its way on to here, get ready to go viral – especially if yours involves something that didn't go to plan, like a rogue photo-bomber or an animal taking a dump in the background. This is also the place to come for cracking celebrity selfies. Remember that Ellen Degeneres Oscars snap? The one that was retweeted over three million times? Yeah – this is where you find those kinds of selfies, too.

With over three million followers, @HilariousSelfies stays true its biog when it says it's your '#1 source for hilarious selfies'.

Tip: Selfies are a big talking point. This account won't be relevant forever but it's great to jump on trends when they're kicking off, and to be the curator of something that people across the globe are involved in and searching out.

84.
@DRESSEDANIMALS
Founded: August 2014
Following: 240

Whether it's a rabbit in a trolley or a dog dressed in drag, animals are where the LOLs are at on Twitter.

If you work for a brand, utilising the power of a cute pooch could be the key to unlocking massive engagement rates – just be sure to keep it relevant.

But instead of spending hours searching Google images looking for the perfect picture, this account curates the very best of pets on the net. Surely this says it all:

Tip: Everyone loves animals, but unless you use them in a way that's relevant to your brand, you can't expect your Twitter handle to stand apart from the rest.

85.
@HassanRouhani
Founded: May 2013
Following: 267,417

In a flagrant display of hypocrisy, the President of Iran – a country where Twitter is banned under his administration – has a Twitter account, and you can find him on @HassanRouhani.

His Twitter presence has, for obvious reasons, been received with a mix of intrigue and disgust by the media, other Twitter users, and even Twitter's Chief Executive @DirkCostello and Twitter co-founder @Jack.

@DirkCostello sent him a message saying 'Mr. President, enjoying your Tweets from the UN. We would love the Iranian people to enjoy them as well. When will that be?', while @Jack inquired 'Good evening, President. Are citizens of Iran able to read your tweets?'

@HassanRouhani actually responded to @Jack, saying: 'Evening, @Jack. As I told @camanpour, my efforts geared 2 ensure my ppl'll comfortably b able 2 access all info globally as is their #right.'

Keep an eye on how this unfolds. It will be interesting to see whether the Iranian people get to enjoy the same level of freedom as their President anytime soon.

Tip: If you're going to ban people being from being on Twitter, perhaps don't advocate the channel yourself – or at least, expect the stick.

140 ULTIMATE TWITTER LOLS

4.
The Art of the Troll

Lurking under Twitter's metaphorical bridge live the villainous trolls. Learn how to handle them and learn from their mistakes.

86.
@JamesBlunt

Founded: October 2009
Following: 885,260

Life's too short to take yourself seriously, so laugh a little and get in there with a self-deprecating one-liner before someone else does. Or at least that's the ethos of singer @JamesBlunt.

Earlier this year, Blunt released his latest album, Moon Landing. Now, although the record sold well, his return to the charts was less than well received on social. But it's what he did with this negative reaction that has turned him into one of Twitter's biggest heroes.

When he sees negativity directed at him, he retweets the offending message, adding his own acerbic one-liner into the mix. Like this:

- And no mortgage. RT @hettjones: James Blunt just has an annoying face and a highly irritating voice
- Viagra and coffee mostly. RT @paigefergg: Bloody hell why is James Blunt still going

Imagine being that unwitting average Joe who has a pop at Blunt, only to have the man himself retweet you and turn your poor attempt at a joke into something genuinely funny that people want to share and talk about. Truly devastating. Well done, Blunt. I might even buy your album for this one. Or at least troll you on Twitter until you publicly shame me.

Tip: If you're quick (& thick skinned!), you can own the conversation.

87.
@KTHopkins
Founded: February 2009
Following: 227,109

Katie Hopkins found fame on reality TV show *The Apprentice*. But unlike most former reality stars, who fade into obscurity after their 15 minutes in the spotlight, she's gone on to carve herself a successful career as an infamous rent-a-gob. It's not just This Morning and Channel 4 panel shows that have provided her a platform to air her (largely) offensive views, however. Hopkins is Queen of vitriolic tweeting, and uses the social media site to preach her opinions on everything from parenting issues to immigration.

For divisive characters like Hopkins, who specializes in 'fatshaming' and verbally attacking celebrities (she once labeled singer Lilly Allen 'a short ass mother in big pants', for instance), Twitter can be pretty dark place. For every person who agrees with her, there are countless others who think she's a complete moron. And they have no problem in letting her know it!

But, like a bully, the more reaction she gets, the more controversial she becomes. By fueling the Twitter fire, everyone's inadvertently fueling her controversial career.

There's something satisfying about seeing people speak out against her, though.

Tip: If you hate trolls, stop fueling the troll fire.

88.
@NigelTheGoat
Founded: May 2012
Following: 141

In a world filled with trolls, there's a lot to be nervous about when entering the social space if you're already in the public eye.

But when it comes to levelling harsh words at celebs, no one delivers a scathing put-down quite like @NigelTheGoat. This guy's got trolling down to an art.

Depending on your view of Twitter-based harassment, this is, arguably, one of the most underrated accounts out there. Sure, he's only got a few hundred followers, but this goat is comedy gold.

Here's an example of the grief he's been giving the lads over at @BBC5Live:

• Useless football team lose match. Cue a stream of morons on @bbc5live

• #BBC5live the three stooges are giving us the benefit of their opinion. God help us.

• #bbc5live Great, after the shouting commentators, we now have the drunken moron 'phone in'! Terrific!

• He literally has no filter. Give him a follow for all the things you want to say, but would never dare.

Tip: If you don't like it – Twitter gives you the opportunity to voice your opinion and give real time feedback.

89.
@RealDonaldTrump
Founded: March 2009
Following: 2,709,167

You don't become a billionaire without pissing a few people off, right? This badass billionaire loves nothing more than ruffling a few feathers on Twitter.

His is narcissistic, hyperbolic tweeting at its best. Trump trumps up on topics ranging from foreign affairs to the economy, which at face value seems a bit dry. However, the man is completely without filter, and that means this stuff is (often inadvertently) very funny.

His tweeting highlight was when @David_J_Roth made up a Donald Trump quote and tweeted it: 'I was never one who looked at success as bad. For me, success was always good. I loved it, and still do." - Donald Trump, *Winning*, pg. 27'

You can guess who retweeted it, can't you? And it gets better. Trump hasn't even written a book called *Winning*.

Better still, Trump wasn't even tagged in @David_J_Roth's original tweet, which can only mean one thing – he was searching his own name on Twitter, and in doing so, appropriated a made up quote from a complete stranger.

Tip: If you're big-time enough for people to quote you, only retweet quotes you have actually said.

90.
@SouthamptonFC
Founded: June 2009
Following: 280,441

As the old adage goes: 'ask a stupid question, get a stupid answer'. And the same is true of Twitter. If you say something stupid, prepare for suitably silly replies.

The social media team at @SouthamptonFC are great at hunting down fans who've made a bit of a tit of themselves on Twitter, and often take the opportunity to score points (if you pardon the pun) with their followers by turning these comments into an opportunity to showoff their funny side.

Here's an example of a conversation they had with one fan:

•29: Pause in play with Sinclair down for treatment, so a few #SaintsFC players taking on some fluids. Humid night in the Netherlands. [0-1]
•@SouthamptonFC how do u know all this
•@charliehard1 Erm, we're at the game. #SaintsOnTour

Needless to say, the "Erm, we're at the game" got more favourites and retweets than the score update.   They're great at gently mocking their fans, and getting involved with the sort of banter football nuts love, but don't necessarily expect from the club they support.

Tip: Don't take things too seriously on Twitter. Instead of getting frustrated, just make a joke of it.

91 & 92.
@RickyGervais @TheTweetOfGod
Founded: February 2009 / October 2010
Following: 6,245,772 / 1,628,341

If you're on the fence about comedian @RickyGervais, checking out his Twitter profile will ensure you fall off on the right side. Now this is a man who can whip the Twittersphere into a frenzy with a single tweet, simultaneously invoking admiration and disapproval. Watching him press people's buttons is one of the greatest joys of Twitter.

When Gervais fans feel put off by his tweets, he likes to push them a little further. Here's a great example of that:

• 'Complaining about what someone tweets about is like calling up the numbers in classified ads and shouting "But I don't want piano lessons!"'

So what happened when wind-up merchant (and outspoken atheist) Gervais crossed paths with @TheTweetOfGod?

This parody account took Gervais in his stride, and where other than Twitter could such a magical conversation unfold:

• @RickyGervais: ". @TheTweetOfGod what did you, as your son, get you, your own dad, for Father's day?
• @TheTweetOfGod: "As my own son, for Father's Day I bought Myself a necktie. And as My own father, I thanked Myself and silently felt disappointed yet again."
• @TheTweetofGod: "By the way, @RickyGervais, thanks as always for the many prayers you directed My way last night, as you secretly do every night. #Faitheist"

98

- @RickyGervais: "They were for Zeus actually but you just kept listening in."

Then, fellow tweeters joined in on Gervais' religious encounter...

- @ABAOProductions: "Get a room, you two."

Quick to the chase, as ever...

- @RickyGervais: "We tried but there isn't one. We're in a stable."

Tip: Stick to your guns and your beliefs while embracing your fellow tweeters.

93.
@Puma

Founded: June 2009
Following: 959,316

Jean Oelwang (CEO of Virgin Unite) once said 'Businesses don't own brands anymore, people own them'. Now that's something that German sportswear brand @Puma would have done well to remember when it launched its recent #FasterGraph campaign.

The idea was simple, and personalised – two boxes ticked. BUT, they missed a simple yet crucial part of good social practice: moderation. @Puma asked its followers to tweet their favourite Puma-wearing player to get a personalised autograph. To enter, all they had to do was tweet @Puma and a player using the hashtag. What could go wrong?

As there was no one moderating the responses, no one intercepted the followers who had changed their names. An example being: "Liverpool are Wank. Falcao said so."

And if @Puma's social team weren't having a shit day as it is, rather than adding moderation or pulling the campaign completely, they changed the hashtag. Aaaaand, it started again.

Tip: Never underestimate moderating your content especially if it's being pulled through to your website.

94.
@PatrickMarkRyan
Founded: March 2009
Following: 7,818

There are lot of celebrities kicking arse on Twitter by being funny, engaging, and offering an insight into their day-to-day lives. But one of the best things about following your favourite actor, singer, sportsman or reality star is that you can talk to them directly, and even knock them down a peg or two if you want to.

When basketball legend Lebron James (@KingJames) tweeted 'My biggest fear, losing it all', one of his followers, @PatrickMarkRyan replied with 'I have $17.63 in my bank account". This was a great way of letting Lebron know he was being a bit of a douche, and probably gained Ryan a few extra followers in the process.

It's tweets like this that show how free you are to voice an opinion and square up to a celeb. Mind out, though, because if you send abuse a celebrity's way, they might troll you back and retweet you, causing their mega fans to send some hate your way.

Tip: Never slate @OneDirection. Their fans are crazy.

95.
@NoToFeminism
Founded: August 2014
Following: 59,886

Rightly or wrongly, this parody account has built its success on poking fun at feminism. With preposterous statements and abysmal spelling, at face value, this account looks like it's out simply to amuse. However, thanks to its playful, humorous approach, it's become hugely successful.

This account isn't so much a place for debate, but a way of subverting the traditional approach of communicating feminist ideas. By making ludicrously anti-feminist statements, it highlights the stupidity of people who actually think in this way.

Here's a sample of its top tweets:

- I don't need feminism because my sex life is not a political agenda
- I don't need feisnm because these have changed my life i could FINALLY lift a pen and learn to write #blessed
- I don't need fesimnim because I prefer old men to be in charge of my reproductive system it is comforting like putting on grandads cardigan

Tip: Have a unique take on something with a big level of interest, this will get you instant awareness.

96.
@Fart
Founded: March 2008
Following: 75,157

If toilet humour isn't your thing, @Fart offers plenty on non gas-related gags. In fact, the man behind the stinky facade, John Hendren, rarely makes jokes in that vein: his main focus is on trolling the Z-list.

The best instance of this is when @Fart totally owned baldy rapper Pitbull. It all started with a harmless campaign #ExilePitbull, where the star's Facebook fans got to vote on which Wal-Mart they'd like to see him perform in.

@Fart and his partner in crime David Thorpe caught wind of this and spearheaded a campaign to send Pit' to Kodiak, Alaska – a remote island with a population of around 6,000 people. The guys mobilised their Twitter followers and, sure enough, Pitbull had to pack his bags!

But that's not the only time @Fart caused a stink on Twitter:

• is that tweet why the leader of the Catholic Church and earthly representative of God blocked me on a website
• the only time i caught a dude looking at porn at work it was really weird porn like a lady outside peeing on an old tire
• if someone has "freethinker" in their bio that is code for "i'm an atheist or libertarian online and i'm gonna tell you about it constantly"

Tip: Don't be one of those people who retweets the negativity so your fans can troll on your behalf – rise above!

97.
@GaryLineker
Founded: January 2012
Following: 3,207,108

Jug-eared crisp-scoffer @GaryLineker has built a career on playing and talking about football. And although sportsmen aren't known for being the most articulate fellas, Lineker's Twitter account is totes LOLs. He's posted some top-drawer tweets in his time, including, 'Taxi driver just said 'never liked you as a player and not really that keen on you on the telly.' He won't be liking his tip either.'

Lineker has also found himself at the centre of a few amazing Twitter moments. The best yet was the furore around the goatee he sported while presenting Match of The Day's 50th Anniversary programme. Needless to say, the usually clean-shaven presenter's lip and chair hair wasn't well received, and the audience couldn't wait to put their two cents in:

- @Mrbry: When Gary Lineker reaches puberty that goatee beard is really going to come into its own.
- @PhantomGoat: Gary Lineker adds a pencil-goatee and suddenly he looks like an amateur magician.

A big Tweeter with an equally dry sense of humour, Lineker's next tweet was: 'Seems like the overall verdict was great show, crap goatee! It's going.' No hard feelings, Lineker. Just don't grow it again!

Tip: Whatever you do, you won't please everyone. Just be yourself, and feel free to reply and to take action – you can make that conversation yours.

98.
@BoringMilner

Founded: July 2013
Following: 340,057

This has to be one of the greatest sporting parody accounts.

Despite his on-pitch prowess, football talent James Milner has something of a reputation when it comes to post-match interviews. He's dull. Really dull.

Monotone, mundane, and missing a few brain cells, it should come as no surprise that someone has set up a Twitter account called @BoringMilner. This account exaggerates all of poor Milner's most tedious interviews to hilarious effect, and has even surpassed the number of followers the real deal has on his account.

Here are a few examples of just how brilliant whoever's behind this account is at replicating Milner's tone:

- I said to Gerrard It was just like watching Liverpool when you set up Suarez. He said This really isn't the time for Jokes, James. I said Ok
- I've just realised that we played Sheffield Wednesday on an actual Wednesday. You couldn't make it up could you.
- I've got to say, Iran v Nigeria has been the game of the tournament for me. What a belter, it had everything.

Tip: I call this positive trolling; it's done in a harmless way with a spot on tone of voice. Nail the basics with your tone and you'll have nothing to worry about.

99.
@GusTheFox
Founded: December 2011
Following: 105,218

What's not to love about a weird and sadistic fox?

@GusTheFox describes himself as a 'troubled soul', who uses Twitter to boast of the pain he inflicts on other animals. Of course, there was the time he 'punched a hen so hard that the little red bit on top of its head - mohawk/glove? - exploded.' And let's not forget when he 'met a stoat called Robert Towel, who told a wonderfully charming story about the time he visited The Dordogne. I'm going to eat him now.' Charming.

But Gus isn't just any vicious, anthropomorphic fox; he started life on Twitter, and has since launched a website and brought out a book. This fox is big time. He even has a few celeb followers! Well, if you count @RizzleKicks as celebrities, that is.

His account is a great place to hang out for vulgar, insightful and hilarious tweets – and the odd celebrity fact.

Tip: If you're going to troll and that's your thing – at least make it amusing and entertaining for everyone that's following you. This is uncouth yet entertaining, which helps set it apart from your average troll.

100.
@NeedADebitCard
Founded: May 2012
Following: 16,926

It may sound a boring, but some people manage to create really compelling Twitter accounts simply be retweeting relevant content. There are heaps of them out there, but one of the finest examples is @NeedADebitCard.

The person behind this account identified a growing trend among Twitter users for sharing their personal details – specifically (and bizarrely) their debit card details. This account has a simple message: social media is no a place to do this.

@NeedADebitCard searches out people who've publicly shared pictures of their debit cards and bank details online, and retweets them, thereby highlighting how dangerous this information could be if it got into the wrong hands. It's immediate, shocking, and a great way to get over-sharers to see the error of their ways.

If you have a message to get across, this account proves that you don't need to think of original content. You can simply retweet and curate a feed of relevant tweets, letting others do the hard work for you. And achieve Internet infamy at the same time.

How's it trolling? Well, more people can access your card details with every retweet.

Tip: Never share you bank details on Twitter, ever.

101.
@StealthMountain
Founded: November 2011
Following: 26,808

@StealthMountain joined the public shaming game in November 2011. The person behind this account is clearly a nosey bastard (and a pedant to boot), who proactively searches Twitter for grammatical blunders. Now, that would be annoying if it wasn't so funny; the great thing is that they limit themselves to only hunting people down who are guilty of saying 'sneak peak', when they actually mean 'sneak peek'.

For the grammar police out there, you'll appreciate that @StealthMountain tweets everyone who gets it wrong with 'I think you mean sneak peek'. Nothing more. Nothing less.

Tip: Set up a search term for relevant content, whether it's your brand name or something you're interested in – this will help you to find the content that's most significant to you.

102.
@David_Cameron
Founded: December 2007
Following: 813,577

Twitter is an excellent way for MPs to communicate policies and engage their constituents. It's also an excellent medium for the public to let politicians know exactly what they think of them. For better or worse.

As you can imagine, Prime Minister David Cameron's tweets aren't exactly a LOL a minute. But the replies he gets are, such as:

• better than your shite story.
• Boris Pumped Your Bird
• Fuck off dishface...

There's also a lot to be said for the accounts that @Number10Gov has followed over time, too; one such account was @ILikeTitsDaily, which is apparently the 'number one account for hotties with nice boobs'. Yup, this actually happened!

The reason behind this (literal) boob came as a result of some less than social-savvy decisions made by the digital team over at Downing Street. They used an auto-bot account to create the illusion that Cameron's team was actively using Twitter and looking to interact with the community. Auto-bots have no moderation process, and can follow any old account – something that the guys at Number 10 learned the hard way.

Tip: NO AUTO-BOTS, EVER. #DieAutobotDie

103.
@ErasedTweets
Founded: ACCOUNT SUSPENDED
Following: ACCOUNT SUSPENDED

Everyone says things they don't mean, from time to time. The same can be said for when people tweet. Twitter is an immediate platform, with 80% of users accessing it on their mobile[6]. So it comes as no surprise that when people tweet things in a rush, on the fly, they make mistakes.

Thankfully, Twitter has the option to delete tweets. So if there's an embarrassing typo, something's factually incorrect, or you bleed your heart out after a drunken night out, you can delete it and pray no one saw.

@ErasedTweets, however, is not so forgiving. It tracks these tweets down, and takes screenshots of the ones it thinks will cause the most backlash before the unwitting sender has time to repeatedly hammer the delete button.

Once it's on the net, it's hard to take things back. So, like driving, never tweet if you've had a bit to drink – that's where a lot of celebs go wrong.

Tip: Read, read and read again. Are you actually happy with that tweet?

---

[6] Twitter Inc. 2014

104.
@GreggsTheBakers
Founded: February 2009
Following: 89,987

Trolling doesn't just happen to Z-list celebrities. It's something brands have to put up with, too, including delicious pasty-mongers @GreggsTheBakers.

When some nerd hacked @GoogleUK and changed Greggs' slogan from 'Always fresh. Always tasty' to 'Providing shit to scum for over 70 years', Twitter was ablaze with people dissing the Geordie bakers. And a vast number of Twitter users spread the word further by inviting others to Google 'Greggs' and see what came up.

But while the social bods at @GreggsTheBakers were tweeting @GoogleUK for a helping hand, they also took the opportunity to turn a negative into a positive.

Instead of taking things lying town, they responded with wit, and took ownership of the conversation unfolding on Twitter:

- @GreggstheBakers You've not really been providing shit to scum for 70 years, have you?
- @yagretbigwazak we've been serving tasty treats to our wonderful customers for 75 years actually!!!

Tip: Trolling happens! Rise above it and you'll have the power to regain your seat at the table. Panic, and all hell will break loose.

105.
@KyleKinane
Founded: March 2009
Following: 120,698

I like to use the dinner party theory when it comes to social media. It should be an environment where you arrive (preferably with a bottle of red in hand), and enjoy the company and conversation. As the evening develops (and the wine flows), the conversation gets better and you create stronger bonds with the people around you. In the same respect, if there's someone at the party who's gone wild for the wine and they're chewing your ear off, chances are, the next dinner party you're both at, you'll do your very best to sit the opposite end of the table - or in a brand's case, you'll unfollow them.

This is a lesson comedian @KyleKinane wanted to teach brands, because, like me, he wants them to be as human and authentic as possible online, and not become conversation-killing auto bots.

So, how did he do it? Kinane made it look from the outside as though salsa manufacturer Pace Picante (which wasn't an account set up by them, but by Kinane himself) auto-favourited all the tweets that @mentioned them. Brands (and people!) who have this function set on their Twitter accounts usually do it to make their customers feel like they're really engaged with them. Obviously, this isn't a human approach to your social strategy... you see where this is going, don't you?

Kinane whipped up a social storm, firing loads of negative tweets at the brand's fake account; for example, *'I wouldn't rub Pace Picante-brand salsa in my asshole if my turds came out on fire'*, and they subsequently favourited it. Not only did this make the tweets visible to followers, but when Kinane used the account to apologise and make amends by offering free salsa, it made the brand look really silly and inauthentic.

Essentially, he used this as a way of highlighting how brands that do operate in this way should not use social media (even if, in this case, Pace Picante weren't actually behind the activity). In the process, he built up his profile and earned a hefty social following. To date, he's at a whopping 120K followers. Nice one, Kinane... even if it was a weird trick.

Tip: Be human!

106.
@AmznMovieRevws

Founded: September 2014
Following: 40,848

How did this not happen sooner? There is finally a dedicated Twitter account for all those ludicrous, totally bonkers movie reviews submitted by Amazon users: @AmznMovieRevws.

Within 24 hours of launching, this account wracked up a whopping 27,000 followers, which suggests that there's been considerable demand for someone to aggregate this material for quite some time.

The man behind this account literally reads through all of the movie reviews, finds the best one (for all the wrong reasons), and shares it with his community.

This feed is all about the screenshots and the film titles, leaving room for people to add their own commentary.

Tip: Keep your tweets short. Go for 100 characters instead of the full 140 to let people add their own commentary. And, if you're anything like this account - use Twitter as a caption for your pictures.

140 ULTIMATE TWITTER LOLS

5.
Building a Badass Brand
Cut a fat slice of funny pie and tuck into these hilarious Twitter handles

107.
@FatJew
Founded: June 2009
Following: 146,903

Josh Ostrovsky, also known as 'The Fat Jew', is a little bit of everything; he's an actor, a comedian, a writer, a rapper, and a social media legend to boot. Granted, the majority of his posts skew towards to the inappropriate – but you probably got that from the name...

Put simply, this man's life is strange. He was recently paid $1,000 to judge a pregnant women's wet t-shirt competition, for instance.

Through sharing the best (or worst, depending on your outlook) of the 'net, he has become something of a cultural icon. With The Fat Jew, you don't have to trawl the Internet for those LOL-a-minute things to send your pals – he does all of that for you, and more. Here are a few of his best bits:

• Hey rappers on twitter, saying "LOL" in every tweet is about as gangster as two dolphins sitting on a rainbow tongue kissing
• Why do people say "grow some balls"? Balls are weak & sensitive, if you wanna get tough, grow a vagina. Those things take a pounding - @pmxo
• If I ever fuck up a parallel parking job twice in front of strangers i'll just immediately drive to another city and start my life over.

Tip: If you don't have a full team to help create content, there's people out there who curate the good stuff for you.

108.
@LegoAcademics

Founded: August 2014
Following: 42,168

Unlocking the power of Twitter only comes when you can really worm into the mindset of your audience, and work out exactly what makes them tick.

@Lego has a large and very diverse consumer base. Of course there's the kids, but in order to engage its older, nerdier audience, the legendary toy brand created @LegoAcademics.

This account documents challenges from within the science sector in a super fun, visual and light-hearted way, by recreating them using Lego! Is it the 'coolest' account to follow? Perhaps not. But it's certainly one of the most innovative.

The best people and brands on Twitter are storytellers, and @LegoAcademics is brilliant at it. It's simple, effective, and proves you're never too old to play with Lego.

Tip: Storytelling is rife.

109.
@Oreo
Founded: March 2010
Following: 448,567

In today's digital age, where smartphones are on the rise, Twitter has become the first port of call for journalists and members of the public to report news. It empowers everyone to get a message out to the world in seconds. For instance, the siege on Osama Bin Laden's compound and news of Amy Winehouse's death are two major incidents that broke on Twitter well in advance of any news network.

Whether the news is happy or sad, one thing's for certain: it spreads quickly across Twitter. So, if you want your tweet to get noticed, you face loads of competition.

@Oreo has the perfect formula to keep its tweets visible and competitive at times like this. To keep its marketing reactive when major events take place, the brand assembles its crack team of social media supremos (which also consists of designers, lawyers, PRs, and copywriters), and tasks them with posting clever, reactive content.

When the Super Bowl aired in 2013, there was a blackout at the stadium. And it was time for @Oreo to shine! The biscuit makers fired out a tweet within seconds, saying: 'You can still dunk in the dark' with a picture of an Oreo in the dark attached. Proof that this sort of timely content pays dividends, the tweet was retweeted over 10,000 times in a single hour.

Tip: Is your business taking social media seriously enough? If not, it's time they did. Starting thinking about how your brand can be fully involved and own that conversation.

110.
@Mangal2

Founded: June 2010
Following: 14,428

Mangal 2 – a Turkish kebab house in Dalston – isn't just home to North London's tastiest hangover cures. It's also the funniest restaurant on Twitter.

These tweets go some way to proving that fact:

• "Our salad is so well dressed that Tom Ford takes a summer internship here every year to learn a thing or two."
• "Nandos across the road from us. They named their sauce Peri-Peri. No need to say it twice. Attention-whores Attention-whores."

Penned by the owner's son, who has gone on to become the @DailyMail's social media editor, this account works because it's got such a defined tone of voice. Yes, that tone's crude as hell, but it's also entertaining, retweetable, and a great conversation starter. It doesn't matter how many times they say c*nt or insult Dalston's native hipster community – it still helps foster brand affection and put them miles in front of their competitors.

You'll also like @The_Dolphin_pub

Tip: Twitter helps small businesses. It's free to run and businesses can reach thousands, nay, millions of people if they nail their tone. Even if your brand can't afford paid marketing, you can still own the conversation on Twitter with a razor-sharp wit.

111.
@Shitmydadsays

Founded: August 2009
Following: 2,908,789

The brainchild of Justin Halpern, @ShitMyDadSays is an account that tweets exactly that – the unfiltered crap that comes out of Halpern's father's gob.

Proof that this account basically embodies the moans, gripes and bad jokes that fathers everywhere make, here's a few of the most LOL-inducing moments from @ShitMyDadSays:

- "Put the rake down. I don't wanna sit around watching you 'give it your best.' Either stop sucking or get the f**k out of the way."
- "See, you think I give a s**t. Wrong. In fact, while you talk, I'm thinking; How can I give less of s**t? That's why I look interested."
- "Don't focus on the one guy who hates you. You don't go to the park and set your picnic down next to the only pile of dog s**t."

Now, kudos to the kid behind this account; Justin Halpen – the time and dedication to this account has scored you a nice book deal.

You'll also like @AwkGrlPrblms, @Shitnobodaysays and @IrishMammies.

Tip: It takes time to build a community and, for a while, you'll feel like you're talking to yourself. Stick at it – if you're willing to invest time and effort, your community will come.

112.
@Harry_Styles
Founded: August 2010
Following: 22,326,686

He's one fifth of the world's most famous boy band by day. But by night, @Harry_Styles fancies himself something of a philosopher. Styles recently updated his bio to say: 'Looking for gammon, not splinters'. Hardly Plato, of course – but nevertheless, this statement really got his fans thinking.

Harry started trending within minutes. Here's a sample of the tweets that came rolling in:

- "Looking for gammon, not splinters." IT MEANS THAT HARRY LIKES OVERSIZED GIRLS LIKE ME!! HAHAHAHA-HAHAHAHAHAHAHA. #NOHATEPLS
- CHECK HARRY STYLES' NEW BIO DID HE JUST COME OUT OR NAH
- 'looking for gammon not splinters' is basically saying Harry's looking for the strong not the weak I LOVE THIS KID

Harry's fans never got to the bottom of it. But this incident shows how the dedication of "fandoms" on Twitter can turn even the most innocuous of comments into a major online event.

@Harry_Style's biggest fan? That'll be @Livvy_Thompson.

Tip: Unlike many celebrities, Harry still uses Twitter in a genuine (and slightly random) way. He promotes what he's doing to his loyal base in a way that brings them even closer to him, which helps him to build his empire.

113.
@WstonesOxfordSt
Founded: August 2010
Following: 68,967

One way to gain a following on social is by making people feel like you understand them. @WstonesOxfordSt nails this (in fact, the tweet that guaranteed their slot in #TwitterLOLs was when they said 'social media managers need a hug'. Amen.).

This account is quirky, and for brands and people on social, it's hard to define an engaging tone of voice and stick with it. This account is excellent because it's done exactly that.

It's actually a brilliant strategy from @Waterstones, which allows individual stores to setup their own Twitter accounts. With over 20,00 employees, this is a risky strategy.

It's a brilliant example of a brand not taking social too seriously, keeping it simple and timely while engaging a community of loyal fans. This account makes me want to delete my Amazon account and only ever shop at Waterstones, Oxford Street. It goes a little like this:

- I found the apostrophe where I'd seen it earlier. Shivering from the cold, crying from hunger, I gave it my coat and took it in.
- Q: What do you call a man with a book on his head? A: BOOK HEAD. WEARER AND DEFENDER OF BOOKS. #bookjokes

Tip: Nail your tone of voice, keep it consistent and you'll nail Twitter.

114.
@CaitlinMoran
Founded: October 2008
Following: 513,340

@CaitlinMoran is a woman of many talents; she's an award-winning journalist, a best-selling author, and a fearless feminist. She also happens to be a badass tweeter.

In her own words, Moran has been 'writing the fuck out shit since 2002'. In the years since, she's carved herself a niche as the go-to woman for ballsy gags and commentary on everything from LGBT issues to @LadyGaga's boobs. Put simply, she's ace.

She's also a great example of how to maintain a natural conversation with your followers. Although every tweet of hers is golden, it's the witty, personalised replies that make her so special. They never fail to put a smile on your face, and she's testament to the power of making your followers feel valued – her fan base, though not necessarily the biggest, is among the most loyal on Twitter. Here are a few of Moran's most outrageous, yet endearing, tweets:

- I guess it would be "Different but equal to men, and with more shoes."
- Hand-wash your tights in the shower while you've got the conditioner on. And dance to Kate Bush.
- "Feminist" just means "being equal to boys," and wanting to be inferior to boys is the REALLY scary thing.

Tip: Your fans are in control. Respect them, give them valuable insight and you'll build their trust and loyalty.

115.
@Sofifii

Founded: March 2012
Following: 150,288

Next up, it's time to introduce @Sofifii to the #TwitterLOLs stage.

Co-founder of the hugely successful Hello Giggles blog, she's a chick with a flair for witty, mood-lightening one-liners.

With @Sofifii, you'll see the world through the eyes of your not-so-average twenty-something. From celebrities to gossip, fashion to TV – if it's something that inspires a smile, she's tweeting about it.

For an insight on what a tastemaker like @Sofifii makes of the world, check out some of her finest Twittery below:

- I'm sorry but having good posture looks weird
- I need you to respond to my text in either 30 seconds or 24 hours. Everything in between is pointless to me.
- it hurts my feelings when my computer can't do 45 things at the same time.
- I don't feel safe in a home with less than two phone chargers.

Tip: Use Twitter as a tool to promote yourself whilst driving traffic, awareness and buzz to your external site.

116.
@MindyKaling
Founded: March 2009
Following: 3,259,864

If you haven't caught an episode yet, The Mindy Project is a sitcom set in New York City. Its star and writer is @MindyKaling, who plays an uptight, romantically incompetent gynaecologist – and if her Twitter account is anything to go by, she's just as brilliant and barking in real life as she is in the show.

Her Twitter feed is a perfectly crafted extension of the her TV series, and gives anyone hungry for more of Mindy's wacky, boy-troubled humour a place to go when the show is off air. Creative, enigmatic, and passionate, Mindy inspires her followers to be their best and offers ways to overcome all sorts of adversities: from waxing-related disasters to bad restaurant etiquette.

Here are some tweets that prove she's a lady to follow:

• If I was blind I could tell who the hot girls in the nail salon were by how boring their stories are
• David Beckham plays soccer?!
• Oh shit, guys, I'm so excited, no one I saw today will I see tomorrow so I can wear the same outfit again.

Tip: Allow Twitter to be an extension of your personality, this way you and/or your product will still be at the forefront of people's minds.

117.
@ChoupettesDiary

Founded: June 2012
Following: 42,591

Which is stranger: the fact that @Chanel Creative Director @KarlLagerfeld's pet cat Choupette is on Twitter, or the fact that Lagerfeld once proclaimed he wanted to marry her: 'There is no marriage, yet, for human beings and animals… I never thought that I would fall in love like this with a cat.'

Probably both equally odd.

Lagerfeld and his pet puss continue to live in unwedded bliss; however, Choupette's following is going from from strength to strength on Twitter.

@ChoupettesDiary gives followers an insight into the fashion industry through the eyes of a cat. With two maids (one for the day and another for the evening, natch), Choupette spends her day dining with Karl and nibbles from discarded Chanel pieces. This is one fierce feline.

So it should come as no surprise that there's a book deal on the cards, called *The Private Life of a High-Flying Fashion Cat*, in addition to a beauty campaign with Japanese cosmetics brand Shu Uemura.

Tip: If the business isn't right in your name, look around you for what to market and give the most extraordinary of things a voice.

118 & 119.
@OldSpice @TacoBell
Founded: June 2009 / July 2007
Following: 223,782 / 1,399,550

Achieving the same success as your average @OldSpice campaign is every marketers dream. But saying you want your campaign to go viral in this way, isn't the most realistic (or sensible) objective. Before executing a new campaign, you have to be clear of what you want to achieve from the outset... unless, of course, there's the budget to pay for your content to go viral.

In addition to its viral video output, @OldSpice is always engaging, and has a great brand tone of voice, firing out one-liners like this : 'Why is it that "fire sauce" isn't made with any real fire? Seems like false advertising.'

Another brand dominating the social space is @TacoBell, who replied to the above with '@OldSpice Is your deodorant made with really old spices?' This playful feud gave both brands the opportunity to showcase their personalities, while entertaining their followers. It's always great to see brands interacting in this way, giving consumers an insight into the people and personalities behind them. Not only does it make them more relatable, but it puts them at the forefront of people's minds.

Tip: Even brands can show off their personality on Twitter, look for conversations where you can have a valuable input.

120.
@ArenaFlowers
Founded: March 2008
Following: 22,405

Nailing your tone of voice is a one-way ticket to Twitter stardom, and florist @ArenaFlowers has one of the most cleverly scripted Twitter feeds out there.

Like all brands, they've got to get the sales, and if we think about the olden days, broadcasting those sales messages would have been the best option. Now, @ArenaFlowers knew things had changed and took a gamble.

Instead of relying on Valentine's and Mother's Day messages to engage their online community, they created a social strategy with humour and playfulness at its core. The result? A winning account that is read by thousands, and ensures the brand is visible – whether they need flowers or not!

It's fun, light-hearted, and, when they need to, it tweets about its products and deals with customer issues... but never at the expense its distinctive tone. Here are few examples of its bloomin' marvelous approach:

- Jurassic Park is basically a film about an under-staffed IT department.
- The average person swallows ten spiders and three horses a year without realising.
- The Queen refers to coins and banknotes as 'selfies'.

Tip: If your product is straight forward, do something that brings it to life and gives you the opportunity to be at the forefront of the consumer's mind.

121.
@SelfawareRoomba
Founded: June 2012
Following: 23,807

Gone are the days when you cleaned your own floors. We live in the age of the Roomba: a vacuum cleaner that works without human intervention. Set it on a programme, and it's off!

@SelfawareRoomba speaks on behalf of its fellow Roombas, and regales its followers with the problems and objects it comes up against on an average day doing housework.

This account doesn't look like it's been set up by iRobot (the company that makes Roomba vacuums), but it would have been a genius idea if it did.

Tip: Think of a sister account - one which can really bring your product to life. Twitter allows you to give things a voice that wouldn't normally be heard. Did you know, 63% of brands have multiple Twitter accounts[7].

---

[7] Dashburst, 2014

122.
@50shedsofgrey
Founded: June 2012
Following: 109,560

Thanks to the enormous success of E.L. James' erotic Fifty Shades Of Grey trilogy, Twitter is overrun by '50 shades of...' accounts. So getting yours noticed is tough.

@50shedsofgrey is one of the most successful iterations of the '50 shades...' format, and is also the title of a parody novel. It chronicles the journey of a man who is torn between his wife's sexual adventurousness and spending time with his beloved garden shed.

You know it's going to be good when the spoof book outsells the original in just two weeks. #Fact

Here are some of the accounts most shedonistic Twitter moments:

• 'This is a contract between you and me,' she said coolly. I signed shakily. This was it. In twelve easy monthly payments the shed was mine.
• 'Hurt me,' she begged, raising her skirt as she bent over my workbench. 'Very well,' I replied, 'You've got fat ankles and no dress sense.'
• 'I'm a very naughty girl,' she said, biting her lip, 'I need to be punished.' So I invited my mother to stay for the weekend.

Tip: Jumping on a trend will really boost your community BUT you have to make it good, else it'll get swallowed up with all the others.

123.
@RobDelaney
Founded: February 2009
Following: 1,060,493

Social media is a critical tool for comedians. It's not all about the content, but it's a place for them to market themselves and experiment with new material. @RobDelaney owes his meteoric rise up the comedy ladder to Twitter; he's even won awards for his tweets.

In 2010, Paste magazine named him one of the Top 10 funniest people on Twitter. He also became the first comedian to be crowned 'The Funniest Person on Twitter' at the Comedy Central awards with these:

• Probably the worst thing you can do to a person is leave them a voicemail.
• The story of the Titanic speaks to me because I once tripped over a bag of ice at a party & then killed over 1,500 people.
• You can take the boy out of the country but you can't take the country out of the boy because countries can't fit in boys anyway.

Delaney used Twitter as a launch pad, which helped transform him from your average funny guy into a one-man brand. If, like Delaney, you're looking to make Twitter your springboard, here are a few simple steps to follow that'll help turn you into a sell out gig:

• Be genuine. No one likes fake people. Find your niche – Delaney's was obscure humour. And quite a few breastfeeding gags.

- People want to do business with people, not businesses, so start interacting and showing what you've got to offer. If you don't put yourself out there and start talking, you'll go unnoticed.
- Give to people and you too shall receive. Don't hold everything back, otherwise else you won't learn anything new.
- Tweet like a pro – be the expert! Give your community something that they cannot find elsewhere, just like Delaney.

Delaney made it via Twitter, so what's stopping you?

Tip: Well, as above, use Twitter as a Launchpad for your career

124.
@ShitGirlsSay
Founded: April 2011
Following: 1,976,718

Over at @ShitGirlsSay, you'll see gender stereotyping at its funniest.

Masterminded by Canadian writers Kyle Humphrey and Graydon Sheppard, this hugely popular Twitter account has been exploded into a brand, which boasts its own book and a fabulous, gender-bending YouTube series.

Of course, the fact that this account gets its laughs from critiquing women, means it's come under fire from some feminist groups. But it's not meant to be anything subversive – their tweets are just great, satirical observations on the silly things girls (and guys) say:

• Feel how soft my legs are.
• Would you still be friends with me if I looked like that?
• I hate the word "moist"
• I'm never drinking again.
• She could be pretty if she really wanted to.

You'll also like @AverageLifeAims and @JuliusSharpe.

Tip: Think of other platforms to create additional content for your Twitter stream, for example, Vines or YouTube videos.

125.
@ChelseaVPeretti
Founded: September 2009
Following: 344,931

@ChelseaPeretti considers herself 'one of the best comedians out there'. No pressure ensuring that Twitter account lives up to the hype, then.

As a stand up and TV actress (get streaming Brooklyn Nine-Nine, if you haven't seen it), she's a fantastic gal to follow. @ChelseaPeretti keeps it real with every tweet – no thought gets held back. She gives a blow-by-blow account of her manic life, and offers followers a front row seat to her expletive-ridden feuds with the odd rapper or two.

Here are a few tweets that will give you a flavour of just how nuts she is:

• What's that called when you're in your head thinking "do u hate me" every time you're talking to someone? Oh yeah - life!
• EAST COAST U HAVE 5 MINS TO PEE BEFORE @Brooklyn99FOX hopefully don't do it for 5 min straight
• My armpits smell like Burger King
• WHO WILL BE THE GREAT LEADER 2 LEAD US AWAY FROM THE INTERNET

Also, check out @TheMiltonJones and @OC if you like this one.

Tip: Even if you're a person, use Twitter as if you're a business. Promote where you'll be and what you're doing for additional awareness – it let's people feel closer.

126.
@LenaDunham
Founded: April 2009
Following: 1,776,973

For anyone who's been living under a rock for the past few years, @LenaDunham is an American actress, screenwriter, producer and director. And, most notably, she's the creator and star of HBO's critically acclaimed, ratings slam-dunk Girls.

If you haven't seen it (where the hell have you been?), Girls is a comedy about a group of girls living in New York City. It's been touted as this generation's answer to Sex And The City, but with fewer aspirational characters and a stronger sense of entitlement. Moreover, it's rude, bravely honest, and absolutely hysterical.

Dunham's approach to Twitter is much like her series: brutally honest and instantly relatable...

• It's a bummer when you really like a song and then you find out it's by Chris Brown
• Statistic: roughly 90% of the men who call me fat on twitter have a confederate flag as their avatar
• Calling someone a drama queen is so negative. Why not "content creator"?

Tip: On Twitter, if you're being a real person rather than a parody – never be afraid of being human and open. That's the only way to build trust.

127.
@O2
Founded: June 2008
Following: 246,013

When a brand opens up a dialogue with its customers, it can result in all kinds of public relations nightmares. No more so than when a member of a brand's customer care team goes rogue on Twitter and sends inappropriate pictures to customers (this has happened!).

Telecoms giant @O2, on the other hand, gets a butt-tonne of positive PR pick up from the witty back-and-forth between its social media team and the public. This is a company that really gets its customers, and knows it can't just feed them corporate lines to keep them happy. They have to go above and beyond.

Here are a few of the best examples of @O2's social team pumping out fresh, timely (and funny) responses to its customers:

- Customer: "@O2 I haven't had any problems!" @O2: "I've had 99."
- Customer: "Oi! O2! Because of you I missed a call from my dear old mum. For that I think I owe you a pint. Ta! :)"@O2: "Um... you're welcome, we think. But if your mum asks, we'll totally deny this tweet"
- Customer: "@O2 F**K You! Suck d**k in hell" @O2: "Maybe later, got tweets to send"

Tip: Customer service can be really mundane and repetitive. If you're playful and funny – you'll take the sting out the conversation.

128.
@Peperami
Founded: March 2014
Following: 26,995

According to a recent survey, a whopping 76% of people think Twitter users tailor their content to be funny – they want that RT[8].

This is something comedians can, obviously, use to great effect. Hence the number stand-up comics who've become Twitter superstars. Of course, it's much harder for brands to come across so funny, real, and connected.

@Peperami, however, had no issue doing this on Twitter. It launched its Twitter feed in line with the World Cup. All of the brand's content was topical, relevant and funny.

At the same time, @Peperami launched its Vine account (Twitter's six second video service), and used it to create footie caricatures out of its famous meaty sticks. From fans to the ref, @Peperami had every angle covered.

This humorous content earned them another 27K followers on Twitter and the brand's sales increased by 30%[9].

@Peprami's strategy is to be in the moment, and that's how they can entertain and win over their fans. Nicely done, for a sausage.

Tip: Big moments equal big engagement.

---

[8] #TwitterWorks, September 2014

[9] #TwitterWorks, September 2014

129.
@Joan_Rivers

Founded: February 2009
Following: 2,245,287

When @Joan_Rivers died earlier this year, Twitter went into mourning. It had lost one of its brightest stars.

Like most comedians, Rivers used Twitter to promote her shows and personal appearances. But it was also her preferred way of testing some of her more provocative material; she used the site to crack some of seriously inflammatory jokes.

In her memory, here are some of her most offensive (and wonderfully funny) tweets:

- Celine Dion's asking $72 million for her Florida home. For that you get 5 bathrooms and the promise of never hearing the Titanic song again.
- Italy has become so Americanised. I can't believe they're even selling pizza here now!
- I must admit I am nervous about getting Alzheimer's. Once it hits, I might tell my best joke and never know it.

Tip: Use Twitter to test content with your audience, if they're following you – they're a fan already and whether they engage or not will show you whether it appealed to them.

130.
@TheRealPSL
Founded: September 2014
Following: 95,728

It's autumn, which means it's time for Halloween and, more importantly, @Starbucks' limited edition Spice Pumpkin Latte.

To celebrate, the Seattle-founded coffee chain has created a brand new Twitter handle: @TheRealPSL. Not only is this a clever, simple way to create some buzz and raise awareness of the Spice Pumpkin Latte, it's got loads of LOLs going on.

Take this picture it tweeted out, for instance. It plays on the tradition of baristas misspelling people's names on their take-out cups.

It's great when brands can make fun of themselves like the example on the right:

Tip: 53% of people on Twitter recommend product in their feed[10].

_____

[10] Erik Quelman

131.
@KellyOxford

Founded: March 2009
Following: 588,053

This stay-at-home mum's Twitter feed is chock-full of sharp observations on life, pop culture, and parenting. But she doesn't just boast a killer Twitter feed. She's now the proud author of a *New York Times* best-seller: *Everything is Perfect When You're A Liar*. Yup, this lady's Twitter prowess secured her a book deal (and she's since written a screenplay for Warner Bros.).

Strangely, however, Oxford likes to repost her best tweets. Granted, she usually waits over a year to send her finest one-liners back out into the Twittersphere, but it's like paying to see your favourite stand up comedian, only to find they regurgitate the same joke over and again. Keep it fresh, Kelly!

Despite that, this chick's definitely worth a follow. Here are a few of her funniest bits:

- If you can name five Kardashian's but can't name five countries in Asia, stick a knife in a socket.
- Billy Ray Cyrus & Alan Thicke, please pick up your children.
- TIP: If you want to find the biggest asshole at your party, leave an acoustic guitar out.

Tip: Don't repeat your tweets - keep the content fresh.

140 ULTIMATE TWITTER LOLS

6.
Money, Money, Money

Money can't buy you happiness, but it sure as hell can buy you a decent Twitter following

132.
@McDonalds
Founded: September 2009
Following: 2,555,629

So McDonalds ran a campaign called #McDStories, encouraging people to share their happy memories from one of its restaurants. Now, Maccy D's isn't necessarily renowned for its hospitable ambience and flavoursome cuisine, so you can imagine how much fun Twits had with this hashtag. Here are few examples:

- Ordered a McDouble, something in the damn thing chipped my molar #McDStories
- #McDStories I lost 50lbs in 6 months after I quit working and eating at McDonalds
- Watching a classmate projectile vomit his food all over the restaurant during a 6th grade trip. #McDStories'

Of course, in many (most) people's view, this campaign did not go to plan. However, the hashtag trended world wide – which would normally cost a business £500k – so thanks to everyone rushing to take the piss out of old Ronald McDonald, the fast food brand that everyone loves to hate secured itself some major exposure.

Credit where credit is due though, this is an anomaly - usually everything they do in social is hot shit! Google their Angry Bird or Pick and Play campaign, for instance.

Tip: Put yourself in the shoes of your customers. If you didn't work for the brand, how would you respond? What would you think? This doesn't apply to just campaigns; it applies to every message you send out to your customers.

133.
@PaddyPower
Founded: April 2008
Following: 450,307

@PaddyPower is an Irish bookmaker that's become famous for its irreverent tone on Twitter. They're also fans of producing super cheeky ads that get banned.

It's a brand that puts a controversial spin on everything, and there are endless examples of just how entertaining they are on Twitter. However, one of the best instances of its mega-LOL behaviour is this text exchange with Scott...

A guy called Scott, left a bar in Dublin after bagging the phone number of a girl named Jess. Being polite, he dropped her a text. Unbeknown to him, he had the wrong number and was actually texting the guy behind @PaddyPower's Twitter account. @PaddyPower tweeted all the text exchanges and got their community involved with Scott's misfortune: what did they think he should say next? What would they like him to ask?

The conversation was priceless, and seeking audience involvement in this way is key to growing engagement and upping your following. To boost involvement, @PaddyPower added a touch of media behind the tweets to guarantee exposure – a well played move.

Tip: If something is getting great organic engagement and you have an always on strategy for your media, give it a little boost with some additional spend behind it.

134.
@HVSVN
Founded: March 2009
Following: 1,035

If you work in social media for a brand, there's one thing that always worth bearing in mind: you can join the conversation on Twitter, but it should always be based on your customers' wants and needs. You need to help and support them in order to get what you both want.

@British_Airways learnt that they're no longer in control when they lost @HVSVN's father's baggage.

The usual happened, @HVSVN tweeted, tweeted a little more and, yet, he was ignored. Until he paid to promote his tweets, that is.

Promoted tweets are ordinary tweets purchased – usually by advisors who want to reach a wider audience and encourage engagement from their followers. With his increased awareness of @HVSVN's predicament, @British_Airways finally responded, and subsequently found his luggage. This proves the power of paid media as great way of getting you noticed.

Tip: There are several ways to ensure you get the most out of your promoted tweets:

• Drive website traffic by asking users to click
• Drive leads using Lead Generation Cards
• Promote sales and giveaways

NB: *You can always spot a Promoted tweet as it's clearly labelled on the top right-hand corner with 'Promoted'.*

135.
@IanJamesPoulter

Founded: April 2009
Following: 1,768,292

Get your tiny violin out for @IanJamesPoulter: the most followed golfer on Twitter with nearly 2 million followers.

Something bad happened to @IanJamesPoulter recently. While traveling with his family he tweeted: 'Booked 6 business seats for my wife & nanny to fly home & @British_Airways downgrade my nanny so katie has no help for 10 hours with 4 kids.' Poor guy.

When he touched down, the multimillionaire Ryder Cup winner discovered he had created quite a storm on Twitter. There were memes, angry jokes, and, this being Twitter, a lot of people lining up to take a swipe at him. Forget the popular hashtag #FirstWorldProblems, it was then all about #IanPoulterProblems. Genius!

Here are a few of the highlights:

- Tonight please spare a thought tonight for Ian Poulter in his tough time. #pushthroughPoults!
- My heart bleeds for you @IanJamesPoulter. Children are being killed in Gaza and you're crying because your wife has to look after her own

Tip: If you're filthy rich and boast about it, chances are – Twitter will not be your friend.

136.
@Mastercard
Founded: September 2009
Following: 299,411

It's important to keep it real on Twitter; otherwise you can end up with egg on your face a la @Mastercard.

When the finance giant partnered with the BRIT Awards in 2014, the collaboration had huge potential – not least because of all the A-listers set to attend the event, and the resulting press coverage. @Mastercard wanted to ensure it capitalised on the exposure but, unfortunately, the actions of its PR company completely undermined it. They issued journalists with scripted tweets and told them what to say in exchange for accreditation to cover the event. So much for freedom of the press...

As you can imagine, the media fallout was huge:

• "Please fellow journalists do not agree to the absurd conditions for covering @BRITAwards. I've just been told what I should tweet. No."
• "The demands sent by House PR included suggestions for tweets before, during and after the event, all with the hashtag #PricelessSurprises."

@MasterCard also paid to promote the hashtag #PricelessSurprises. This would have cost them in the realms of £500K for a global trend. Advertisers, like @Mastercard, use this promotional feature from Twitter to jump start their conversation but unfortunately, this conversation obviously didn't go the way that the brand expected it to go with tweets like, the following:

• *"Good press coverage is hard to bribe. For everything else there's Mastercard. #PricelessSurprises"*

It's things like this that prove the value of a contingency plan!

Tip: First things first, think about the repercussions of your campaign. How would you feel if you were sent Twitter copy to send out from your channel? Then, think about how you'd respond and use a very good media company who, if things don't go to plan, can pull the media spend as quickly as possible.

If, and only if, you have your audience at the heart of everything that you do, will you have nothing to be scared of.

137.
@BoonePickens
Founded: March 2009
Following: 122,617

Where else but Twitter would an 84 year old manage to own a rapper?

Thanks to its accessibility and immediacy, Twitter serves as a great platform for people of all ages to express their opinions quickly, succinctly, and to lots of people around the world. Oil tycoon T. Boone Pickens worked Twitter to his advantage when he replied to rapper @Drake's tweet 'The first million is the hardest.' Within seconds, @BoonePickens replied, "The first billion is a helluva lot harder". Obviously, the octogenarian transformed himself from fusty old billionaire into a Twitter celeb overnight.

And, @Drake, consider yourself *owned*.

As you can imagine, the pick up with favourites and Retweets was quite something.

Tip: Don't boast. If you want to talk money, I'd recommend using the DM feature (same for long chats - otherwise everyone who follows both of you will be inundated with your tweets in their feed!).

138.
@Charmin
Founded: May 2011
Following: 54,216

75% of people in America admit to using their smartphone while on the toilet[11]. For a brand like @Charmin – one of the United States' leading toilet paper manufacturers – this opens up a world of possibilities.

Introducing, #Tweetfromtheseat:

- #ThatAwkwardMoment when someone suddenly opens your stall door and scares the life out of you #TweetFromTheSeat #Mortified
- #ThatAwkwardMoment when your little one decides to announce he's done. In public. Out loud. #TweetFromTheSeat

@Charmin's social strategy isn't about sales, but building brand affection. Its #Tweetfromtheseat campaign also keeps Charmin at the front of people's minds when, well, they are most likely to thinking about loo roll. While it can't directly measure the impact of sales by having an engagement-only approach to social, its staff can leave the office knowing that they've put a smile on the faces of bum-wipers around the globe.

Tip: Getting the right hashtag is an art, not a skill. Think of something that memorable, unique, and perfectly sums up the main principles of your campaign.

---

[11] Digital Spy, 2013

139.
@ElizabethHurley
Founded: December 2009
Following: 462,384

Yes, it goes against the rules of Fair Trading, but the simple fact is that some celebs get paid to tweet. Trouble is, not only is it pretty obvious when someone posts tweets they've been compensated for, but they also face getting sued.

Considering the number of actions brought against celebrities who've done this in recent years, it's unsurprising that @ElizabethHurley is currently in breach after tweeting 10 references to @EsteeLauder's product range. She's been the cosmetic giant's brand ambassador for 17 years and, yet, still fails to make her tweets look natural enough to go undetected by the authorities. Careless, Liz. Careless.

She should take note of @KimKardashian's commercial prowess and savvy tweeting. Apparently, the reality TV star and owner of the world's most famous backside made a whopping $10,000 for tweeting about a product to her millions of fans and got away with it.

Tip: If you're in a position where you're getting paid to tweet, add 'ad' or 'spon' into your tweet and you'll have no legal bods on your back.

7.
Only on Twitter...

140.
@brinaliscious
Founded: April 2010
Following: 1,748

I mean, just wow:

SabingBing @Brinaliscious   775d

Did they come up with 911 as the police number after 9/11 ? #wondering

Follow

Tip: Think before you tweet.

140 ULTIMATE TWITTER LOLS

Acknowledgements

First and foremost, I think you (Yes, YOU!) need to be acknowledged. Thanks for sticking with me to the end of this not-so-hefty tome.

Next up, it's the parents. Good ol' Gaz (the anti-socialist) and @MichelleBeswick. Without them, I wouldn't have been able to supply the world with yet another book to read while on the toilet.

In all seriousness, they stuck by me and taught me that you can chat about these things all day, every day but it's harder (yet possible) to actually do something about it.

My baby bro, @CamBeswick, who, when I told him what I was doing literally fell off his seat in hysterics, saying: 'You're making a picture book?! Is that because you can't read?' Cheers bro!

My partner, @SAMMCLONDON, who's not only been in the firing line for all the moaning, late night Twitter stalking and, well, a generally boring couple of months as I've wanted to lock myself away in order to get this thing written. But he's also done a lot of the design work, so thank you.

In order to actually get this out the door, I pulled a few, slightly enormous, favours. So first up, Ben Piears – thank you for taking the time to read this book when it was in its infancy, and telling me that I'll get there. Whether I'm ranting or raving, you've had my back and offered me input every step of the way.

140 ULTIMATE TWITTER LOLS

@GavJewkes, my delightful editor. I genuinely could not have done this without you. You are (and always have been) on my 'one to watch' list. I am in awe of your quick-wit.

@RiRoDoodles, the illustrator. C'mon – isn't she amazing?

@James_R_Hart, my #mentor, and Nick R for teaching me the art of being a 'doer'. Your support from the second I walked through ASOS' doors has been incredible, and I cannot express how grateful I am.

Now, a massive thumbs up emoji to everyone else who's chipped in along the way, @helanda99, @BassJustin, @annarclaudia, @HughjWoods, @ASOS_Hannah, @Martyn, @Paul__Armstrong, @NataliePead, @BarryMCosmestics, Andrew Magowan and Stu Mears.

Glossary

- @ - an '@' sign calls out users on Twitter

- # - a hashtag, used to search relevant content or terms

- @Username – a username is how you identify someone on Twitter

- Accounts – people who are set up on Twitter

- Auto-bot/Twitterbot – a programme used to automate posts, for example following accounts or hitting favourite on a tweet.

- Analytics – the numbers involved in measuring the success of your tweets, or social content

- Bio – your bio is a short description that appears within your Twitter profile to personalize your account and to create your Twitter persona

- Block – if you block a user they'll be unable to view your content or get in touch with you

- Bug – an internal error, this will need to be fixed by Twitter (I recommend tweeting @Support)

- Crowdbooster – a third party tool to measure the success of your social content

- Deactivation – when someone deactivates his or her account (you can reactivate if you want to start tweeting again!)

140 ULTIMATE TWITTER LOLS

- Direct message (DM) – a private tweet, only visible to the person you've tweeted. You must be following the person to send them a DM

- Discover – surfaces personalized content based on your interests

- Emoticons/ emojis – pictures and characters

- Engagement – an engagement is when someone interacts with your content, for example favourites your tweets or follows you

- Favourite - Tap the star icon and the author will see that you've liked their tweet

- Follower – subscribing to a Twitter account

- Geolocation – showing in real-time where you sent your tweets from

- Gif – an animated picture

- Hacking – Gaining unauthorized access to a Twitter account

- Hashflag – a hashflag is a specific series of letters immediately preceded by the # sign which generates an icon on Twitter such as a national flag or another small image

- Hashtag - a hashtag is any word or phrase immediately preceded by the # symbol. When you click on a hashtag, you'll see other Tweets containing the same keyword or topic

- Header photo - your personal image that you upload, which appears at the top of your profile

- Home - home is your real-time stream of Tweets from those you follow

- Hootsuite – a third party tool used to track your Twitter conversations

- Lists - from your own account, you can create a group list of other Twitter users by topic or interest (e.g., a list of friends, coworkers, celebrities, athletes)

- Meme - an Internet meme may take the form of an image, hyperlink, video, picture, website, or hashtag. It may be just a word or phrase, including an intentional misspelling

- Mentions - mentioning other users in your Tweet by including the @ sign followed directly by their username is called a "mention." Also refers to Tweets in which your @username was included

- Notification - the Notifications timeline displays your interactions with other Twitter users, like mentions, favorites, Retweets and who has recently followed you. If you request it, we send notifications to you via SMS or through the Twitter for iPhone or Twitter for Android apps

- Parody - you can create parody accounts on Twitter to spoof or make fun of something in jest, as well as commentary and fan accounts

- Promoted tweets/accounts – putting money behind your tweets or your account for additional

- Pinned tweets – you can pin a Tweet to the top of your profile page to keep something important to you above the flow of time-ordered Tweets

- Profile - your profile displays information you choose to share publicly, as well as all of the Tweets you've posted. Your profile along with your @username identifies you on Twitter

- Promoted Accounts - promoted Accounts present suggested accounts you might want to follow as promoted by our advertisers. These appear in your Home timeline, and via who to follow, search results and elsewhere on the platform

- Promoted Trends - promoted Trends display time-, context and event-sensitive trends promoted by our advertisers. These appear at the top of the Trending Topics list on Twitter and elsewhere on the platform, and are clearly marked as "Promoted."

- Promoted Tweets - promoted Tweets are Tweets that are paid for by our advertisers. These appear in your Home timeline, at the top of search results on Twitter and elsewhere on the platform, and are clearly marked as "Promoted."

- Protected/private accounts - Twitter accounts are public by default. Choosing to protect your account means that your Tweets will only be seen by approved followers and will not appear in search

- Reply - a response to another user's Tweet that begins with the @username of the person you're replying to is known as a reply. Reply by clicking the "reply" button next to the Tweet you'd like to respond to

- Reactivation - you may reactivate a deactivated account within 30 days of the deactivation date. After 30 days, deactivated accounts are permanently deleted

- Retweet (RT)- the act of sharing another user's Tweet to all of your followers by clicking on the Retweet button

- Scheduled post – a tweet that was created in advance and using a third party, set to a timer to be tweeted

- Service level agreement (SLA) – the time in which it takes you to respond to tweets

- SMS - Short Message Service (SMS) is most commonly known as text messaging

- Spam - refers to a variety of prohibited behaviors that violate the Twitter Rules. Spam can be generally described as unsolicited, repeated actions that negatively impact other users

- Suspended - suspended accounts have been prohibited from using Twitter, generally for breaking Twitter Terms of Service

- Timeline - a timeline is a real-time stream of Tweets. Your Home stream, for instance, is where you see all the Tweets shared by your friends and other people you follow

- Timestamp - the date and time a Tweet was posted to Twitter. A Tweet's timestamp can be found in grey text in the detail view of any Tweet

- Trends - a Trend is a topic or hashtag determined algorithmically to be one of the most popular on Twitter at that moment. You can choose to tailor Trends based on your location and who you follow

- Troll – someone who causes hurt or upset on Twitter by deliberately provoking people

- Tweet - a Tweet may contain photos, videos, links and up to 140 characters of text

- Tweet button - anyone can add a Tweet button to their website. Clicking this button lets Twitter users post a Tweet with a link to that site.

- Twitter - an information network made up of 140-character messages (including photos, videos and links) from all over the world

- Verification - a process whereby a Twitter account receives a blue check icon to indicate that the creator of these Tweets is a legitimate source. Verified users include public figures and those who may have experienced identity confusion on Twitter

- Viral – a tweet that gets a high pick up in terms of engagement and something that has mass conversation online

References

- Sprinklr, 2014 - page 18

- Twopcharts; a third-party site that monitors Twitter Activity - page 32

- Mention, 2014 - page 33

- Image, Twitter.com/Budlight - page 43

- Twitter Inc. 2014 - page 61

- Erik Quelman, NEW FACT - page 68

- Image, Twitter.com/DRESSEDANIMALS - page 89

- Twitter Inc. 2014 - page 110

- Dashburst, 2014 - page 130

- #TwitterWorks, September 2014 - page 138

- Image, Twitter.com/TheRealPSL - page 140

- Digital Spy, 2013 - page 152

- Image, Twitter.com/brinaliscious - page 156